THINKCAT

THINKCAT

An owner's guide to feline psychology

David Taylor

Dedication

To all the cats at present in my life: Sidney, Golda, Sam, Mitzi and
Muffin, Niki's Cagney, Fiona's Tilly, and, in Mallorca, Sue's fine
bunch of shorthairs, *los cinco muchachos negros*.

First published in Great Britain in 2004 by Cassell Illustrated,
a division of Octopus Publishing Group Limited
2–4 Heron Quays, London E14 4JP

A CIP catalogue record for this book is available from the British Library.

ISBN 1 84403 243 4

Produced by SP Creative Design Ltd
Wickham Skeith, Suffolk, England
Editor: Heather Thomas
Designer: Rolando Ugolini

Printed in Spain

Contents

Preface   6

Introduction   13

Part 1
Feline behaviour   19

Part 2
A cat's life   55

Part 3
Problem behaviour   89

Part 4
Training the cat   145

Final thoughts   187

Appendix   188

Index   189

Useful addresses   192

Preface

A day in the life of the Thinking Cat

Cats are crepuscular by nature, tending to be mainly out and about in the twilight hours of dawn and dusk. The typical domestic cat will be roaming the house or outside, courtesy of a cat flap, seeing things clearly with his enhanced vision – the movements of moths, small rodents, early-rising birds and, of course, other cats. If food is left down for him overnight, he will do most of his eating between the hours of 4am and 8am. Cats can be trained to sleep during the eight hours that their owners spend in slumber. Calling or enticing your cat inside before you go to bed, locking the cat flap, not leaving food down after he has had supper and then preparing his first feed of the day when you get up, will quickly accustom him to the regime. It is wisest, particularly with young children around, not to allow cats to sleep in beds other than their own selected places or sleeping baskets and boxes. Cats, like any animals that live close to the ground, sniff each other's backsides, investigate drains and can be too intimate with germ-bearing rodents. They can transmit infections to humans if draped across your pillow for eight hours a night.

Cats need more snooze-time than eight hours, however. They sleep, on average, sixteen hours out of every twenty-four. Cats do not think proactively if placed in a stimuli-free laboratory chamber, but in real life their world teems with stimuli, things to think about and react to, even when they are asleep. While they sleep, their brains continue to function at a basic level, recording and analysing stimuli from their surroundings. In deep sleep, amazingly, the cat brain remains as active as when awake and the senses continue to scan for any sign of danger. At the first sign of alarm, the ever-alert nervous system rouses the body muscles instantaneously. As in humans, their sleep patterns embrace periods both of deep and light sleep: 70 per cent is light and 30 per cent is deep, with the phases alternating.

Yes, the cat does dream. Electro-encephalographic studies have shown that cats dream during the deep phases. Dreaming is often accompanied by external signs that you may observe – movements of paws and claws, twitching ears, flicking whiskers and, in some cases, little noises. What science cannot tell us, of course, is what they are dreaming about. The young female kitten next door, catching that cheeky squirrel that teases him each day from the apple tree? Who knows?

After the first meal of the day, the Thinking Cat will usually go off for a morning nap. This can last into mid-afternoon and is undertaken in some chosen spot, sun-warmed in summer and fire or radiator-warmed in cold weather. Some individuals, instead of slumbering for long periods at a time, go in for a series of cat-naps, but the total sleep time always adds up to around eighteen hours a day. Why they need so much sleep, we do not know. Perhaps the lifestyle of specialist hunters that need to conserve their energy for brief, athletic, high-performance bursts of energy demands all this rest and recreation.

On waking, it is time usually for more nourishment before going walkabout. Adult cats are best fed two to three times a day, and senior citizens three to six times. Dried food can be left down all day and is particularly suitable for use in warm weather when there are flies about. Water, of course, must be permanently available, even though many cats do not seem to drink much. Among the domestic cat's wild relatives, probably only the Sand cat is able to survive permanently without the need for water. It gets sufficient moisture from the meat and blood of prey and conserves its own body water highly efficiently. Cats often surprise us by preferring to sup from a greenish puddle of rainwater or a flower vase even when there is fresh tap water in their bowl. It's a question of taste. Particularly in cities, such as Manchester, where mains water contains a noticeably high level of chlorine, the taste puts cats, and some humans, off. Lucky fussy cats in such areas prefer bottled mineral water.

Time for a stroll, some light exercise, to see what's going on. The Thinking Cat doesn't go in for strenuous exercise. He seems to keep in fine condition just be stretching his muscles every now and then. Essentially a leisure lover, the feline equivalent of a French *boulevardier*, he tends to shun all work and cannot be prevailed upon or instructed, like the dog, to earn his crust. Apart from rodent hunting, which anyway is sport, he does not build lodges like beavers, nests like birds or great apes, or go tunnelling like the mole. He spends much time looking, observing and contemplating. The Thinking Cat wisely, unlike his owners, affords time to just stand and stare.

Once outside, the first stop might be at the goldfish pond to weigh up his chances. The domestic cat is the only member of the genus *Felis*, which includes the European and African wild cats, the Desert cat, the Sand cat and the Black-footed cat, which eats fish. He is fairly adept at hooking fish out of shallow water. Other wild cat relatives that are keen fishermen are the Fishing cat of the Far East, which also uses its paw to scoop out fish and occasionally actually dives in, and the jaguar, which cunningly lies on the riverbank and taps the tip of its tail on the water surface. Fish that sense the vibration of the tap think it is caused by seeds falling from overhanging trees and rise to consume them. A quick flash of the jaguar's paw and it is they that are consumed.

Moving on from the garden pond the cat may well pause to munch some blades of grass and then swipe at, down, chew and swallow a passing housefly. Chewing grass is not, as often supposed, a sign that Tom is feeling unwell. It is good for cats, containing certain useful vitamins, and it also acts as an emetic, helping the animal regurgitate unwanted matter such as furballs. Another popular myth is that 'cats which catch flies go thin'. Not so. It is possible that a cat eating a bluebottle might take in disease-causing bacteria and occasionally worm eggs might be carried by flies from one cat to another, but the risk is minute.

As the cat promenades, he may meet another cat and an investigation of one another will proceed. If he comes across a human, a friendly cat will usually utter a cry of greeting. He is seldom asking for anything, just saying 'how do you do' and the voice is not strident or imploring but may be rather muted and diffident in a shy cat. Suspicious, particularly feral, cats will not greet you in this way but, after halting in their tracks to weigh you up, run off at high speed. If you come upon them in a tight corner, the only sound they emit is likely to be of spitting.

Where now? Perhaps the hedge in the adjoining field. As he goes along the stand of shrubs and weeds he checks out the scent marks of the tom living three doors away whose territory this is. Luckily the marks are at least twenty-four hours old – not likely to bump into the irascible, battle-scarred Ginger, then. A robin flies down to perch on a branch three metres away. He eyes the robin as it eyes him. Not worth launching strike. No element of surprise. Distance instantly computed as too far single pounce. Ignore the provocative bird and move on.

vivelling ears pick up the faintest of rustling sounds in the sun-dried grass to his left. His stereophonic ability pinpoints the origin and distance of the sounds, his eyes focus, unblinking, pupils wide, on the place. There! Something brown, largely concealed beneath a dock leaf, moved slowly from left to right. The Thinking Cat's computer whirrs silently. OK! Pounce now six centimetres to the right of the dock leaf edge and he will intercept it precisely. Crouch, quick waggle of bottom and *go*! The cat's front paws, claws completely extended, land squarely on the back of a field mouse. Simultaneously the cat delivers the killing bite. This bite is far more interesting than you might imagine. The canine, or fang, teeth of all cats, from moggy to puma to tiger are adapted in size and shape to the neck vertebrae of their principal prey species. They pierce between the vertebrae, instantly dislocating them and severing the spinal cord. All of this is done automatically in a split second. The cat does not have to feel here and there with his teeth for the right place – he knows. The teeth of the domestic cat, particularly the fangs, are equipped with lots of special 'pressure feeling' nerves. When the teeth, through these nerves, sense they are in the correct position, an ultra-fast message is sent through special high-speed nerves to the jaw muscles which, possessing an exceedingly short contraction time, pull the jaws together like a highly sprung mouse-trap. Which they are! Having pawed at the tiny corpse for a few moments, the cat, not in a hungry mood, moves on, his brief moment of sport over.

The cat, when walking, moves the front and back legs on the same side simultaneously. The only other animals that do this are the camel and the giraffe. When he runs, he can touch twenty-seven miles per hour, not up to the greyhound's forty-five or the cheetah's sixty-three. Cats only exert themselves when they must. They conserve their energy, barely sweat and only occasionally pant. Their panting is done at a rate of approximately 250 pants per minute. There is no gradual increase in frequency. A cat either pants at the aforementioned rate or not at all. When it is necessary to lose excess heat, in hot weather or after physical exertion, he does so by radiation from his body surface, which is much larger, compared to his bulk, than is the case with bigger creatures, such as the dog or the horse. Cats thus find it easier to dispel unwanted heat.

Moving back towards his home, the cat stops to pass urine. He decides to do it, spraying backwards as usual, against a familiar fence post where it will serve as his marker along with the vertical scratches he left yesterday. His urine can be two-and-a-half times more concentrated than a human's, an adaptation to the high-protein feline diet that produces much nitrogenous chemical waste.

His internal clock now tells him it is time to pop in to see the lady who lives next door. She will be back from work by now. The cat knows the routine. Over the fence, no need to worry about trespassing, as the lady does not have a cat of her own, and her garden, along with his own, has long been accepted by the local cat population as his unquestioned domain. The garden on the other side of his is another matter, it being a no-go area for any of the Cat Town boys and girls on account of a German Shepherd. One jump and he's on the friendly lady's kitchen window ledge. She's washing up and hasn't seen him yet. Best to give one greeting call. Fine, she's looked up, smiling and is, as he anticipated, now opening the window. Right on time, the saucer of food is in its correct place on the floor. Not having a cat, the lady doesn't buy cat food, but she provides all manner of delicious snacks for her visitor, things he doesn't get at home, or, if he did, he would sniffily reject. Being a cat and capricious as cats are, her morsels of bacon, boiled ham and Kentucky Fried are gobbled down here, just as if he didn't receive ample, nutritious, well-balanced food at home. This 'snacking on the quiet' is one of the common causes of obesity in what an owner considers to be a judiciously provided-for puss.

Leaving the neighbour's house, our cat decides to cross the road and visit the nearby smallholding. He jumps over a narrow stream, pauses briefly to watch a frog take refuge under the waterweed, and then continues walking through a thin copse of oak trees. He knows the area well for cats have been shown to be able to construct and remember mental maps of their surroundings. The copse is commonly owned territory for all the neighbourhood cats. Suddenly, our cat stops dead in his tracks. A round, black and white face is peeping out from behind a tree trunk in front of him. Another cat! Who is it? He approaches it quite slowly in cautious but friendly mode with his tail held high in a greeting posture. The other cat stands motionless, adopting a similar attitude. Now the mutual investigation begins.

With heads and necks extended and crouching slightly, they bring their noses together but don't quite touch them. They sniff. Our cat's sense of smell reports that, although the other individual is a stranger, it is a nonthreatening, neutered tom. Next they proceed delicately along each other's neck and flank – more chemical information is obtained. It is now time to sniff the stranger's bottom; very important. As one cat moves to do this, the other tries to do likewise, but because each animal wants to do this before allowing his own fundament to be checked out, it results in them moving in a tight circle. If one cat is more dominant than the other, the subordinate puss may hiss and warn off with a paw strike, and if the boss cat persists in pursuing his anal investigation, this may lead to a fight erupting. On this occasion, our cat is plainly the dominant party, but not minded to press matters further. The stranger crouches submissively and then finally creeps away.

This type of behaviour, a sort of up-close and personal identification parade, is typical of cat socializing. It is known that cats will recognize and pay attention to model cats, cat silhouettes and the mirror images of themselves and will start the same ritual, sniffing the nose and then the anus, and quickly lose interest when they realize that no smell means they have been duped.

After the black and white has departed, our cat typically sniffs the ground where it had been crouched for a final consideration of the newcomer's odour. 'Yes, definitely castrated male, not very old, newly arrived in the vicinity, apparently pacific by nature, at least today, and had just finished a meal of sardines. Must find out what, if any, his home territory is.' He stalks off through the undergrowth.

At the edge of the copse he stops again and defecates. It is one of his favourite 'toilet points' near an overturned rusting wheelbarrow. As usual, as a kind of olfactory calling card, he leaves the faeces uncovered for the enlightenment of the next cats to pass by. Cats often leave droppings uncovered in this way when passing motions in places outside their home territory. In his own garden, however, he would not dream of doing such a thing and always studiously buries both urine patches and faeces. Thinking cats of all species do not like to soil their own doorsteps; they are far more fastidious than dogs.

It's late afternoon: time to go home and take another long nap. His owner will put yet more food down for when he awakes. Then it is play time. Although the cat seems, as we have seen, to keep fit with minimal exercise, playing with your pet, whatever its age, is very beneficial. For permanently housebound adult cats, a climbing frame and scratching post should be provided and regular, best of all daily, playing periods arranged. While the cat is in the house, waking or sleeping, he does not seem to be disturbed by music from the radio or CD player. Even heavy rock is heard with impassivity while he sleeps. It seems likely that the ears and brain of the Thinking Cat can filter out unwanted sounds in the background, rather as we, but far more imperfectly, can concentrate on a one-to-one conversation amidst the din of a cocktail party. Many people believe, and I am inclined so to agree, that cats like good music and leave the radio on for them during the day. A favourite, apparently, is Classic FM. Mozart, Haydn and Chopin, it appears, can soothe the feline breast.

Evening brings one of the cat's favourite times of day. Moths, frogs, toads, hedgehogs, mice, bats and roosting birds are about – plenty of items for the Thinking Cat to watch, if not to seriously hunt. Instinctively, with only the occasional exception, he is wise enough not to tackle certain species of toad that secrete from their skin a toxic slime, nor to tangle with those long-haired caterpillars that can also produce similar irritant chemicals.

So ends the day. No erotic encounters: he was neutered long ago. No scrapping this time with the obnoxious Ginger. One field mouse vanquished. Stomach replete. The cat retires to his favourite indoor spot to sleep, perchance to dream. And think.

> *The cat went here and there*
> *And the moon spun round like a top,*
> *And the nearest kin of the moon,*
> *The creeping cat, looked up.*
> W.B.Yeats, *The Cat and the Moon*

Introduction

I've met many thinkers and many cats, but the wisdom of cats is infinitely superior.

Hippolyte Taine, French historian and philosopher

How cats view the world

As he hogs the prime spot by the fireside, diligently exhumes the bulbs you so carefully planted last weekend or yet again spends too much time wagging the bottom and treading the ground before launching another futile charge at the knowing magpie swaggering across the lawn, what is your cat thinking? How does he see the world you both live in? Why and how does he respond to that world? The aim of this book is to understand what it means to be a cat. To enable you, doting owner of one ingle-nook familiar or curious lover of all things feline, to think cat – like a cat thinks.

The way in which cats behave is, as with all animals, a function of their essential nature. A cat, whether battered neighbourhood tom, formidable Bengal tiger or elusive Amur leopard – under the fur they are all remarkably similar – is by far the most specialized and highly adapted hunter/killer of land mammals. Some mammals are vegetarians; others are omnivores, eating meat or vegetables as available; some are scavengers happy with chance morsels, dead or alive, of animals or plants; and then there are the carnivores, those that principally hunt for and eat flesh. Dogs, otters, badgers, skunks, bears, weasels and hyaenas are carnivores, but ones whose diet sometimes includes non-meaty items. Generally the canine species are gregarious creatures that go a-hunting in packs though there are exceptions. The wild cats, however, are out and out pure meat-eaters, and most of them search out and bring down their prey alone. They are quintessentially self-reliant individuals.

To do this, they have evolved complex physical and behavioural attributes, a process that took many millions of years. Their domestic cousins, descended from the smaller species of wild cat, still possess most of these ancient attributes, albeit somewhat softened and modified in certain respects by contact with mankind and his abode over the past 12,000 years or so. They are still individualists but, like my cats at feeding time, rather more human-reliant. Nevertheless, when Muffin, my beloved puffball of a Birman, prepares, wide-eyed and tense, to pounce ferociously on the pen with which I write, I glimpse the shadow of his forefather, a wild cat of Asia, ambushing a mouse-hare in the bleak Afghanistan mountains.

Cat thought is reactive, a response to stimuli received from the world around it. Put a cat in a stimulus-free environment (an experiment that has been done, but one of which I rather disapprove) devoid of sound, light, touch and smell, and measurements of its brain waves with an electroencephalograph show no activity. That cat apparently does not reflect on why it has been so treated. Human beings under similar conditions can think proactively and spontaneously without stimuli, pondering, wondering, creating thoughts although, after some time experiments show, psychosis sets in. So now we know: cats can't compose poetry. But what they can do they do exceedingly well.

The thinking of a cat is dependent upon its intelligence being informed through a range of highly tuned senses, some far more sophisticated than ours. The brain processes the information obtained, not just through learnt knowledge but also by instinct, the genetic product of aeons of evolution. And when the thinking requires action, the cat's body is a perfectly designed hunting machine, ready and waiting to go.

When you've read what follows and understand more of the thinking of the cat, what use will it be? Certainly you will get more enjoyment out of your pet as you watch for and interpret its now explicable daily doings and, with any luck, for cats, far less than dogs, give little away, you may be able to communicate better with this most rewarding of companions. Will it help you train your cat – to fetch newspapers, as a police cat or guide-cat for the blind? Hardly, but in certain basics, hopefully. Cats, as they would be the first to tell you, don't relish being performing animals. (I say this with feeling, having had to treat circus tigers and lions for many years.) Training is for dogs, horses and dolphins, so my feline familiars intimate. Cats do their own thing – with style.

The family tree of the Thinking Cat

The modern domestic cat (*Felis catus*) is the product of millions of years of evolution. As the age of the dinosaurs drew to a close some sixty-five million years ago, the first mammals – small, tree-living and insect-eating – made their appearance. Some of these eventually evolved into meat-eating carnivores called creodonts, our moggies' earliest forebears. Having rather tiny brains, creodonts weren't very bright and gradually died out around ten million years later but not before giving rise to a much sharper, bigger-brained carnivore, the miacid. All modern carnivores, dogs, wolves, foxes, mongooses, civets, etc., are descendants of the miacids. The cats probably arose from ancient civets. Forty million years ago *Proailurus*, a half civet, half cat creature was around. Unlike true modern cats, which walk on the tips of their toes, it moved along placing all its foot bones flat on the ground. Fifteen million years later, an animal that was mainly cat and only a little bit civet, *Pseudoailurus*, made its entrance. It was the first almost true cat and it went a-walking on tiptoe.

The fossil record tells us that by twelve million years ago the first true cats were swarming across the globe. In Northern Italy and Central Europe, the Tuscany lion and Cave lion, together with giant cheetahs and lynxes, roamed the lowland forests and alpine heights. In China lived giant tigers and cheetahs, and huge jaguars padded through the North American woodlands. As well as these bigger felines there were also various smaller wild cats, including the manul, still to be found in Iran, Afghanistan and Tibet, and around the eastern shoreline of the Caspian Sea, and the now extinct Martelli's wild cat. The latter inhabited much of Europe and parts of Asia and it was most probably the direct ancestor of three modern wild species, the Forest wild cat (*Felis silvestris*), the African wild cat (*Felis silvestris lybica*) and the Asiatic desert cat (*Felis silvestris ornata*).

The domestic cat in Europe and America arose, it would seem, from the crossing of these species. The original tame cats were almost certainly tabby-marked and very similar to the wild cat that just survives in lonely Scottish forests. The African wild cat is larger and stockier than the modern moggy, with a light or orange-brown coat and narrow dark stripes. Found in the forested regions of Africa and Asia, it is even said to hang out still in parts of the holiday islands of Majorca, Corsica, Sardinia and Crete. A solitary, nocturnal hunter, and wise with it, the cat steers well clear of the suntan-oil brigade.

Other domestic breeds outside Europe similarly developed from small African or Asian wild cats. Abyssinian, Burmese and Korat cats still retain many of the physical characteristics of their wild ancestors, such as the Jungle cat of the Middle East and Asia. Modern longhaired breeds have an ancestry that most likely stems from the wild cats of Iran and Afghanistan.

Today's breeds

Thousands of years of cross-breeding led to the wide range of breeds and colours available today. The chance creation of mutations over the ages produced hereditary oddities, such as squint, stumpiness or absence of tails, polydactyly (a larger than usual number of claws) and duplicated earflaps. Some of these quirks are now the main features distinguishing certain breeds, such as hairlessness in the Mexican hairless cat and the lack of a tail in the Manx. The origin of that most superior of cats, the Siamese, is however, wrapped in mystery. We know of no wild feline that might lay claim to being the country cousin of a breed so unique in appearance, voice and behaviour.

So, after countless millennia of infinitely slow evolution, Nature has presented us with its dazzling array of modern wild cats, some perilously close to extinction in our lifetime, ranging from the majestic tiger and lion to the small wild cats which particularly interest us here. The biological processes of natural selection and survival of the fittest, first elucidated by Charles Darwin, have resulted in all cats having skills and attributes tested, selected, honed and fine-tuned by their family tree over aeons.

Domestication

A relatively recent occurrence, domestication was only partly due to Mother Nature. Interaction with human beings was, of course, the main factor. Taming any wild cat, making it biddable (in so far as that is ever possible with the proud cat!) and reducing its aggressive potential (hopefully!) cannot be done, even with the smaller wild species, simply by food and kind words. Even after years in a zoo, a little Rusty-spotted cat, weighing a mere one kilo, must be tranquillized by a flying dart if I am to handle and examine it without being seriously injured.

Domestication of the small wild cats began about 12,000 years ago when man changed from wandering hunter-gatherer to more static farmer, and towns and agriculture were first established. The earliest domesticated species were food animals – cattle, sheep, pigs and goats – as well as dogs, which were accustomed to living in packs and thus adaptable to human society, and first used for guarding and hunting. A principal area of animal domestication was the Middle East, from the coasts of the eastern Mediterranean across to the Caspian Sea and the Arabian Gulf.

With the first farms came grain crops and granaries to store them in. Wild mice and rats naturally took advantage of this bounty, moved in, and were soon followed by predating small wild cats of the neighbouring countryside. As rodent control operatives in their grain stores, the cats were probably at least tolerated by early farmers. It is likely that tamer individual cats (that is where Mother Nature's natural selection mechanisms continued to influence events) stayed near man while those of a wilder temperament felt uneasier and less able to adapt. When, after time the tamer strains were fairly well established in and around the farms, kittens could have been taken and raised in the home, thereby accelerating the progress towards true domestication.

Around 6,000 years ago, the position of cats in Egypt, perhaps the most important country at that time in the Middle East, made a quantum leap forwards when they became venerated cult objects. Female cats were deified as sacred to Bast, the goddess of fertility, and males likewise in relation to the sun god, Ra. All cats in Egypt became semi-divine, the keeping of them was widespread and there were even vast cat cemeteries. By 2900 BC, cat keeping had reached Greece, and 600 years later there is evidence of it in India and China. Eventually, after the Romans conquered Egypt, they brought domesticated cats to Europe and by 1600 BC they had arrived in Britain.

After dogs were first domesticated, artificial selection by selective breeding by man took over from Nature in developing a wide range of different types or breeds. For centuries, dogs have been 'shaped' by their owners to perform certain specific tasks – as hunters, retrievers of fallen game, pursuers of small game underground, fighters in old blood sports, guards of property, pullers of loads, etc. Eventually, with the coming of dog shows, the breeding of dogs to obtain purely aesthetic effects arrived. Today's dogs, basically all descended from wolf-type ancestors, can be seen in a bewildering spectrum of shapes and sizes.

Cats, on the other hand, were not purpose bred for different kinds of work and the concept of selective breeding to produce pedigrees with different colours, designs, and, in comparison to dogs, relatively modest changes in shape or size, did not start until the mid-nineteenth century. (Although the first recorded cat show was held as part of an English fair in 1598, serious showing only began in 1871 with a great event at London's Crystal Palace). Consequently, all cats are, more or less, still cats.

I will defend to the death my belief that all cats are equal. Each is a personality. Each brings delight, friendship, style. There are marginally better or worse mousers, there are more or less pronounced xenophobes, but, by and large, a cat is a cat is a cat with a full measure of the species' abundant virtues and rarely any vices. It is true, of course, that if all cats are equal, some are more equal than others, and, in my case, the self-appointed exceptions to the rule are the Birmans.

1

Feline behaviour

The thinking of the cat is reactive, predicated upon the receiving of information from the world around it. The messengers bearing that information are the cat's senses: seeing, hearing, smelling, tasting and touching.

The eyes of the hunter

Cats clearly need good eyes. And they have them. Their large, gleaming, beautifully coloured irises, vertically slit pupils and intense gaze are a prime part of feline attraction. The cat eye is anatomically very similar to that of the human, but there are some important differences in the ways in which certain structures function, as we shall see below.

Night vision

Cats are said to be able to see in the dark. Not so. In a totally blacked-out room a cat can see no better than you or me. What it can do, however, is gather and magnify the faintest quantities of light in its surroundings. Even on a moonless night the sky is never completely void of light. Faint starlight or pale reflections on high cloud are always present and the cat's eye is designed to gather and use such minute scraps of luminosity.

It possesses a light-intensifying screen composed of up to fifteen layers of cells containing glittering, iridescent crystals, the tapetum lucidum, set behind the retina. This screen reflects every speck of light after it has been detected and then passed through the layers of sensitive rods and cones, so that it hits the latter for a second time so doubling the effect. Cats can make clear visual discrimination at one-sixth of the light levels required by human beings. Their night vision is on a par with that of those other nocturnal mammals: the bat and the badger.

The tapetum lucidum is what makes a cat's eyes flash fire in the dark and probably inspired William Blake's famous lines 'Tiger! Tiger! Burning bright, in the forests of the night'. It is absent in humans who consequently waste much of what little light is around at night, unless they are soldiers using 'starlight-gathering', image-intensifying weapon scopes. Human eyes do not gleam in the night; the red glow of our pupils sometimes seen in flash photography comes from blood vessels behind the human retina.

Nocturnal creatures

And the reason for cats' enhanced ability to see in dim light? Because these animals are nocturnal or crepuscular (active in twilight). They tend to sleep by day and hunt their prey when the latter come out of their hidey-holes – after the sun has gone down. My Birmans, like most domestic cats, follow this pattern of behaviour, napping during the day and scoffing most, but not all, of the food I put down between midnight and 6am.

Cat and human eyes both have rods and cones in their retinas. Rods are receptors that function at low light levels and are also sensitive to sudden movements. Cones are for daylight use and are colour receptive. Cats possess more rods than cones in comparison to humans and therefore have better nighttime and motion vision than us, obviously invaluable when spotting a mouse flitting through the grass in the wee small hours. We know that cats can see colours but not as well as us. They can register purple, yellow and, best of all, blue and green, while red, orange and brown are probably seen as shades of grey. On the other hand, their black and white vision is better and they can distinguish up to twenty-five different shades of grey. This facility may be linked to the fact that their natural prey – mice, rats, voles and other small mammals – come with various light grey, grey-brown and dark grey colours of fur.

The pupil of the domestic cat's eye is round in dim conditions but constricts in bright light, first to a vertically elliptical shape and then, in intense brightness, to a narrow slit. The advantage of having a slit pupil lies in its ability to close more completely and efficiently than a round pupil, such as that of the dog or human being. This serves to protect the highly sensitive retina.

Visual field

Cats are somewhat near-sighted, understandable in animals that need to concentrate on small prey animals close to them. Distant objects, certainly those over about 150 metres, most probably appear fuzzy and rarely interest them.

They do have a wide angle of view which is considerably better than ours. We have a visual field of about 210 degrees of which 120 degrees is binocular. The total visual field of cats is 285 degrees, 130 degrees of which is binocular. Binocular vision, the ability to see three-dimensionally, is highly important to hunting animals, enabling them to judge depth and distance with accuracy when they are about to launch an attack. However, they are not quite as good as humans at estimating range.

Cats are more strongly attracted to quick movements across their field of vision than to vertical ones. Note how your puss will pounce or strike like lightning at a ball rolling across the floor in front of it. It is rather less quick to respond to objects going up or down. The reason is that it is instinctively triggered by anything moving over the ground like its natural prey, the scurrying mouse. And mice are rarely to be seen levitating.

A cat's view of the world

So let's sum up how our Thinking Cat views its surroundings. Concerned with what is happening close at hand and disinclined to appreciate the broader vistas of distant landscape, he sees the world in tones similar to those of a black-and-white photograph which has been lightly touched up, as used to be done sometimes in the days before colour photography, with a palette of pale watercolours by an artist who forgot to bring along paints of the warmer, red end of the spectrum. In addition, the detailed design of things nearby is effortlessly perceived. Cats, in other words, see very well, but differently.

I suppose if cats were employable they would be very good at doing intricate, fiddly things – watch-making, assembling computer chips, maybe even filling teeth! On the other hand, if they could drive, it would be best to steer clear of them; their poor long vision might cause some horrendous shunts on motorways!

The second most important sense

Hearing well is vital to the cat. It does it better than you and me, and, again, in some respects, differently. With a penchant for hunting in darkness, the first sign to Felix of a mouse in the hedgerow or a vole in the standing corn may very well be the faintest rustling sound. Ears before eyes then.

The outer 'funnel' of a cat's ear is far more than just a kind of ear trumpet. Thirty muscles move it as compared with six in man, and a cat can turn its ears precisely to locate a sound far faster than a dog. The inside shape of the outer ear, which is irregular and asymmetrical, combined with the ear movements, produces variations in the quality of received sound waves which enable the animal to pin-point the source with great accuracy. The large echo chambers built into the cat's skull that magnify sound, assist excellent hearing. Over 40,000 nerve fibres link the feline ear to its brain as against 30,000 in man, and this enables a cat to hear well over a range of ten octaves. Man can span only eight.

At high-sound frequencies, the cat's hearing ability is much more acute than that of man or dog and, of course, it is in the high frequency range that you find the high-pitched squeaks and trills emitted by tiny prey animals. Very clever! At these high frequencies, cats, remarkably,

Word recognition

Cats do, as we all know, recognize their names and other words uttered by their owners, particularly at mealtimes. The names of proprietary brands of cat meat are often instantly acknowledged, and a sound such as the click of a refrigerator door can evince a most dramatic response. My Birman, Sidney, will rapidly surface from the deepest slumber if my wife says the magic words 'Bring me the ball'! (There does seem to be a bit of dog in Birman cats!) Overall, however, the feline vocabulary of human words never grows as large as that which is generally learned by dogs.

can discriminate between notes even when there is no more than one-tenth of a tone in difference between them.

As with us, cat hearing declines with the passage of time, sometimes beginning as early as three years of age, and usually with a distinct loss of hearing being evident by the time a cat is four to five years old. White cats, particularly ones with blue eyes, tend to carry a genetic fault that causes deafness. The highly delicate mechanisms of the inner ear degenerate and there is no treatment for this form of deafness.

A sense not to be sniffed at

Smell is another sense of prime importance to the domestic cat (oddly enough, those mighty hunters, the tigers, are thought to have little or no sense of smell!). You and I carry around five million 'smelling' nerve receptors in the membrane lining our noses. Cats have in the region of nineteen million, and a long-nosed breed of dog like a German Shepherd as many as 147 million. Cats insist on smelling things – food, unfamiliar objects, traces of urine and rubbings left as territorial markers by other cats and, of course, bottoms. The odour-emitting glands, situated around the anus as well as on the head of cats, seem to convey interesting information that we humans have yet to de-code.

The feline sense of smell is clearly highly developed and far more sensitive than our own. Food from a newly-opened tin that is eagerly consumed this morning is sniffed at and rejected with a dismissive flick of a paw this evening. It looks and smells the same to me, but apparently it doesn't smell the same or as appetizing to my cat. Cats are especially sensitive to odours containing nitrogen compounds. When meat or fish begins to 'go off', it emits such chemicals, at first in amounts detectable by the feline but not the human nostril. The cat family by nature are carnivores which demand fresh meat with the emphasis on fresh. Not for them the delights of a carcase starting to putrefy under the African sun that draws the keen attention of that other carnivore, the hyaena.

If nitrogenous odours turn cats off, there are other 'pongs' that very much turn them on. The herbs catnip and valerian contain an essential oil, the odour of which can drive a cat into ecstasy. A major constituent of the oil is trans-nepetalactone, a close relative chemically to a compound secreted in the urine of a female cat (queen) when she is on heat. So catnip is a very sexy plant – to cats – and they will respond to it by rolling luxuriously in it (or against the sort of toy containing catnip that can be bought in pet shops) and displaying the kind of typical behaviour usually seen in a queen in oestrus.

Flehmen

There is another phenomenon, perhaps a sort of 'super smell' related to the nose of felid animals. Called flehmen, this consists of raising the head, slightly opening the mouth and wrinkling the upper lip and nostrils in a curious grimace. Watch out for it in your pet. All cat species do it, although it is often not very pronounced in the domestic cat. You will probably see it when yours sniffs at a patch of urine or some strongly smelling substance. One of my Birmans does it with gorgonzola but not, so far, with any other kind of cheese.

At the front of the roof of the mouth of many mammals and some other types of animal, there is a tiny, built-in, glandular sac known as Jacobson's organ. You won't be able to see it. It is lined by receptor cells and opens into the mouth through a minute duct. Its function is not really understood by scientists. In humans it is only a vestigial, non-functioning scrap of tissue, but in the cat family it is a working structure and the act of flehmen seems, in some way, to be associated with sexual matters and feeding. Certainly, nerves lead directly from the organ to areas of the brain concerned with these functions. Perhaps it analyses smells in more detail than the nose, or it may concentrate them. We don't know. Flehmen can be observed at its best in snakes where Jacobson's organ apparently analyses 'smell molecules' in the air that are picked and delivered by the flicking, forked tongue.

The tasty cat

Cats certainly have taste. As owners know only too well, they are the fussiest of eaters, gourmets rather than gourmands, and tending towards the fickle, the prima donnaish, in their acceptance of foodstuffs. Of course it is infuriating if your beloved moggie greedily gobbles down the new brand of cat food with which you have presented him, only to find the following day, after you have returned specially to the shop to purchase a gross of the stuff, that it is now rejected as indignantly as if you had put down a saucer of iron filings.

This type of behaviour, which is common, is, I feel, caused by us humans. If, like me, you are always proffering new samples of food and special 'treats', running, in other words, a cat delicatessen, you are creating a spoilt pet, a fussy pussy. After all, there are lots of cats that happily scoff Bloggs Komplete Kat Kubes or whatever day after day for the whole of their lives. Well, I'm afraid that I won't change my ways. I prefer to spoil and, as a consequence, cat meals at our house are colourful, variegated, serve-yourself buffets of hopefully delectable nosh. Spoilt cats of this ilk are not cheap to run.

A sweet tooth

Cats generally do not possess much of a sweet tooth and some are unable to digest sugars, including the lactose in milk, getting diarrhoea if they consume much of it. Dogs have 'sweet' receptors in the taste buds of their mouths; cats don't. At one time it was thought that while dogs definitely do possess nerve pathways between tongue and brain that can carry 'sweet' messages, cats did not. Now we know that a few 'sweet' bearing nerves do exist in domestic cats and the numbers of them seem to be on the increase! Probably the breeding of cats that share the homes and habits (and tidbits) of their human companions, is stimulating, through natural selection, the use and persistence of such structures. Maybe one day all cats will be Jelly Baby addicts.

Loss of taste

Newborn kittens have a well-developed sense of taste but, as with us humans, the acuity diminishes gradually with age. A temporary loss of taste and an accompanying loss of appetite can occur in cats that are afflicted with respiratory illness, such as feline influenza, just as our taste buds are affected by a bad head cold.

I have known several domestic cats, particularly Siamese and Burmese, which had a sweet tooth. One of mine adored raisins and another regularly went crazy for slices of juicy tangerine. Some wild cat species also like sweet things from time to time. For instance, Manchurian tigers love to eat sweet nuts, berries and fruit in the autumn. In Malaysia, tigers are keen on the durian fruit, and the Flat-headed cat is very partial to sweet potatoes. One assumes that in all these cases the sweetness of the food items is recognized and appreciated.

The touch of a cat

Touch is another sense that is important to the cat although, at least in the case of adults, it is not vital. Newborn kittens are blind, without a sense of smell and with undeveloped ears. To them, touch is a powerful key sense that guides and reassures them when locating their mother's nipples at feeding time. They respond to the vibrations produced by the queen purring as she lies on her side, and it is interesting to note that feline mothers stop purring as soon as the kittens begin to suckle. As we shall see later, rubbing, bumping and sensuous body contact all play a big part in feline behaviour.

Sensitive whiskers
A specially developed area of touch in the cat is associated with its whiskers. Their function is not yet fully understood; something to do with touch for sure, and removing them can distinctly disturb a cat for some time. I think there is no basis for the common belief that a cat's whiskers protrude on each side to a distance equal to the animal's maximum width, rather like a measuring stick, so allowing it to gauge

whether or not it can pass through a given space without touching anything and maybe making a give-away noise when stalking prey. Nevertheless, in the dark, the whiskers serve as immensely sensitive and rapid-acting antennae. The whiskers' owner uses them to locate and identify things close by that it cannot see, much like the way a sealion, searching for fish in deep, dark water, points its whiskers forwards to serve as delicate probes. It is thought that if a cat's whisker touches a mouse in the dark, the cat reacts with the speed and lethal precision of a mousetrap. Some scientists have speculated that a cat may bend some or all of its whiskers downwards when jumping or bounding over the ground at night. Certainly the little desert jerboa uses two of its whiskers to do this, using them to detect stones, holes or other irregularities in its path. Even when this rodent is going at full speed, it can take avoiding action while in the air or on the ground by changing direction in a split second. Maybe cats can use their whiskers in a similar way. As for the Rex breeds of cat with their curly-wurly, often brittle, whiskers, they seem to manage life just as well as the more luxuriously moustached makes of moggy.

The warrior cat

To watch a cat preparing to launch an attack on a mouse in the hedge, a sparrow pecking at seeds on the lawn or just a ball of wool that you conveniently dropped into harm's way is to see a master hunter in action. Cats of all species use their speed and agility over relatively short distances while the canid family – dogs, wolves, jackals, etc. – though slower, have more stamina and can keep going, sometimes for hours, gradually wearing down their target prey.

The fastest cat is, of course, the cheetah, which has been clocked at over 96 kph (60 mph) across level ground. The smaller Caracal lynx can, in certain circumstances, rival the cheetah in swiftness, and its agility is such that it has been known to kill up to ten of a flock of feeding pigeons before they could fly up and away. Domestic cats couldn't come close to such a performance; they more resemble their mighty cousin the tiger in being expert at ambush and the short, sharp, accurate strike, reactive thinking of the highest order on display, though they are not as good stalkers as most of the big cats.

Hunting technique

The prey-catching behaviour of the domestic cat has been extensively studied and is a perfect example of feline hunting technique. Once the cat has, via its senses, detected the presence of prey, it immediately takes advantage of any cover available. Pressing its body close to the ground, it moves forwards, at first quite swiftly, in what is termed the 'slink run'. Then comes a pause. The cat, still flattened, is in 'ambush' position, staring intently, eyes open at their widest. A second slink run and ambush often follows, but if the cat is already close enough to the target, it will commence the final stalk, advancing slowly to the last available bit of cover. The cat pauses again in final ambush. Now the hunter limbers up for the pounce. The hind feet begin treading movements, the tail tip twitches, and the eyes follow the prey's every movement with maximum intensity. When the moment is right, although, as I said earlier, some cats tread and twitch in ambush for too long, the cat breaks cover, sprinting across the ground, body usually still flattened and then, when within reach, launches forwards on the prey, forequarters raised, but with hind legs planted firmly on the ground to ensure stability.

The lethal bite of most cats, wild or domestic, is classically to the neck. I have had two friends killed by neck bites from tigers, and Roy, of the famous illusionist duo, Siegfried and Roy, some of whose white tigers have been patients of mine, was recently seriously mauled about the neck by a young tiger. The neck bite is accurately aimed and usually the two upper canine (fang) teeth pass between two vertebrae, forcing them apart and severing the spinal cord. The paws may be used to help pin down the prey. If the prey animal is relatively large, does not immediately succumb or tries to defend itself, the cat, particularly if a novice or of rather a diffident nature, may release it, reconsider, and then launch a new attack. A more macho, experienced character will retain its grip, rake powerfully with the hind feet, and keep on biting until all resistance has gone.

The domestic cat, leopard and puma, despite widespread belief to the contrary, will never attempt to jump down on prey from above. Instead, they jump down close to it and then launch an attack only when sure that their feet are planted firmly on the ground. Paws are also used either as soft clubs to push down a rodent that has reared up defensively, or to winkle out a small prey animal that has taken refuge in a crevice.

Catching birds

I am pleased to say that my five Birmans are models of incompetence when it comes to hunting and catching birds. My wife swears she has, on several occasions, heard a snigger emanating from a robin on our garden lawn when yet another far too delayed and over-planned attack was launched towards it. Unfortunately, there are many domestic cats around who are exceedingly skilled in bird nabbing, and the annual loss of songbirds through cat predation across Britain is alarmingly high. Catching birds demands different skills and strategy from those employed in hunting small mammals. The feathered prey creatures possess a wide field of vision and are ever alert and on the lookout for danger. Concealment up until the last possible moment is the cat's main tactic. After spotting a likely looking sparrow or even pigeon, it will either run very quickly and then hide a short distance from the target or creep slowly towards it, utilizing cover all the while. Flattening its body to the ground as it advances helps to reduce its profile where cover is sparse.

When the cat is within pouncing or short charge distance of the bird and still in cover, it will stop and stare intently at the intended victim. Then when the bird turns its head away from the cat or is distracted, say, by pecking at seed on the ground before it, the warrior strikes. Of course, the best laid plans o' cats an' men gang aft a-gley, as Robert Burns probably meant to say. Attacks frequently fail, with birds warning one another by means of urgent alarm calls that cats are about, but the commonest reason for a debacle, I believe, is the cat waiting too long and the unwitting bird flying away before the cunning plan can be put into operation. Among the wild feline species, the margay, or long-tailed spotted cat of South America, is one of the most skilled bird-hunting specialists.

Cats bearing gifts

Cats frequently like to bring their kills home. Country cats, in particular, are well known for proudly making an entrance with the remains of a young rabbit, mole or even newt. This 'present' giving is related to the habit of many species of cat of bringing food to their young. In some cases, the beneficiaries can be adult, as with lionesses returning bearing meat for the more idle male. In domestic cats, the bringing of food to the young is not carried out purely by mothers or other lactating females. Females that are not rearing young or males, particularly Siamese toms, will also do it. For many domestic pets, the instinct to satisfy a litter of kittens seems to merge seamlessly into an urge to please the human family 'litter'.

As for you, fond owner who should never look a gift mouse in the mouth, and are the recipient of some small corpse from time to time, it is no use scolding the cat, for it is done with the most amiable of motives. The Thinking Cat is thoughtful, and it is not to be taken as a not-so-subtle hint that your pet is feeling under-fed. Mousing addicts are not starving. As farmers who keep cats in their buildings, as mousers and ratters know, they hunt best on full stomachs. The rodents are pursued as sport; the ancient thrill of the chase still courses in the blood of the humblest house cat. Rodent hunting does carry its risks. Cats are likely to pick up parasites, such as tapeworm, and infections, such as Salmonellosis, from tangling with rats and mice. Although difficult to arrange, particularly in out-of-town cats or cats who are allowed to wander freely from home, do your best to prevent it.

Fighting

The other aspect of the warrior cat's life is the cat fight. Kittens practise their martial arts as play and adults do battle, as we shall see later (see page 134), over territorial rights, ownership of property and in matters of sexual rivalry. Domestic cats rarely kill their opponent outright during fights, but the injuries inflicted frequently lead to disease. Avoidance of cat fights is one of the major reasons for careful owners not letting their pets go a-wandering, particularly at night. A recent survey in the United States showed that the life expectancy of domestic cats that are allowed freely out of the home is two years while that of cats that don't leave the property is fourteen years. Motor vehicles are the Number One contributors to these statistics, but the consequences of battling on the rooftops, and infections acquired thereby, come second.

Cats in the balance

The cat is equipped with an exquisite sense of balance that does not require it to actively think. The tom sauntering elegantly along the top of your garden fence is ruminating about the meal he is going to cadge from your neighbour, not about falling off. If I tried to do something similar I would be ungainly, wobbly, tense and apprehensive. And I would almost certainly take a tumble. Cats detest any sign of instability under foot and they do appear to be thinking when they delicately test an unfamiliar branch with a tapping paw to see if it will take their weight, but the balance mechanism, which constantly monitors and adjusts as necessary the cat's body position, requires no active thought. It is incredibly sensitive, efficient and ultra-fast, acting, far quicker than that of a human, even one as highly skilled as an acrobat or trapeze artist. The system consists of information and commands sent along high-speed nerves linking eyes, inner ears and brain. The eyes register visual changes in the images hitting their retinas which indicate that the cat's posture has altered.

Crystals floating in a tiny liquid-filled chamber in the inner ear are swirled about by changes in the head's position or in its acceleration when moving. The movement of the crystals is detected by sensitive hairs lining the chamber, which, within milli-seconds relay the information to the brain. If, after analyzing the messages from the eyes and inner ears, the brain considers an adjustment in the cat's orientation is needed, it instructs the appropriate body muscles to act at once.

The tail

The possession of a tail greatly assists a cat's balance, although I must say that cats with very short or no tails like lynxes and Manx cats, don't seem to do badly when jumping or branch walking. Tightrope walkers use long poles as counter-balances and the cat uses its tail in a similar way. If, for example, it is walking along a narrow wall and, for some reason, decides to peer over to its left, thereby shifting its centre of gravity, it will automatically swing its tail over to the right, re-establishing its centre of gravity and stopping itself from falling off.

The cat's tail also seems to act as a sort of rudder when the animal is leaping and as a counter-weight when the cat makes quick changes of direction if running at high speed. At each turn, the tail is instantly swung away from the direction in which the body is travelling, thus giving superb 'cornering' stability. No wonder the fastest sprinter among cats, the cheetah, has such a long tail.

Falling cats

The eye, inner ear and brain triumvirate plays a vital role when a cat is falling. Changes in the descending body's position in relation to the ground are computed and then acted upon – all in a split second. First the brain commands the head and neck muscles to put the head 'square' with the ground immediately. Then the rest of the body aligns itself with the head and, hey presto, the cat ends up in a perfect position for a soft landing. This 'righting reflex' doesn't exist in the newborn kitten as it depends on a combination of both eye and inner ear messages. Although kittens are born with a fully functioning inner ear mechanism, they lack the ability to see as their eyes are still closed.

Cats fall usually after being pushed or where the surface beneath them suddenly gives way. It is rarely due, except in animals with middle or inner ear disease, to them simply 'losing their balance'. Cats falling from high buildings have typically been dozing on a sunlit window ledge when somebody inadvertently closes the window. It would seem reasonable to suppose that, the greater the height from which a cat falls, the more injuries, usually in the form of fractures, it would sustain. In other words, the higher, the worse. In fact, the rate of fall injuries does steadily increase the higher the storey from which the animal plummets, but only up to a height of seven storeys. Above that, the fracture rate actually starts to decrease!

The explanation is as follows. After dropping for a distance of about five storeys, the cat reaches maximum speed – the so-called terminal velocity of a falling body. At this point, the speed is constant and thus the inner ear is no longer aware of, and stimulated by, any acceleration. So the cat relaxes and spreads its legs out just as a freefall parachutist does when he is stabilizing his descent, and relaxed bodies are much less likely to fracture (the same broadly applies to infant and drunken adult humans). Threfore a cat is better off being dislodged from a tenth-floor window sill rather than one lower down on the third floor!

Although a falling cat, given the chance in this way, can land reasonably well on all four feet and survive (many do), there is a problem with the head. Because a cat's neck muscles are relatively weak, the head cannot be held back when the animal reaches terra firma but keeps travelling down, the chin hitting the ground with some force. As a consequence, one of the commonest fractures in cats falling from a great height, is of the middle of the lower jawbone.

Can cats super-think?

The extreme sensitivity of cats to sound and vibration, outstripping human capabilities, no doubt explains much of the legendary association of cats and the supernatural. Their reputation down the centuries and across cultures has led to them sometimes being worshipped and at other times persecuted.

Infamously they were implicated in witchcraft, considered to be low-ranking demons sent by the Devil to advise and perform small malicious errands for witches. One of many examples is the notorious seventeenth-century witch-finder Matthew Hopkins who swore he saw a diabolical spirit called Holt, in the form of a little white kitten, visit a suspected witch whom he was interrogating. Absurd and cruel as such beliefs seem today, is it possible that cats really do have some mysterious, albeit benign, powers? Might they, for instance, have a sixth sense? Are they telepathic or psychic? Many perfectly intelligent people believe so, and the internet is packed with web pages describing the telepathic powers of cats and ways of communicating telepathically with them. Unfortunately, there is, as yet, no scientific evidence to back them up.

Telepathic cats?

There are innumerable accounts of cats who seem to know when their owners are on the way home and go to the door or window to await them. Certainly in some cases the cat, with its highly tuned ears, is picking up the first faint sound of the approach of a familiar car engine, but that does not explain the majority of such incidents. Science has no explanation. Could it be telepathy? I know of several instances where dolphins and other animals have exhibited similar inexplicable abilities.

Good vibrations

Like some other species, cats may give warning of an impending earthquake or volcanic eruption. Strange behaviour by house cats was widely reported in the ten to fifteen minutes preceding the disasters at Agadir, Skopje and Alaska in the 1960s. A German biologist present at the 1960 Chilean earthquake described cats becoming alarmed up to sixty seconds before men were aware of the first tremors. Several captive pumas, however, did not appear to notice a thing. Village peasants on the slopes of Mount Etna in Sicily keep cats as early warning devices. When the drowsing fireside tom ups and makes for the door hell-for-leather for no apparent reason, the human occupants know it is best to follow hotfoot. There is nothing supernatural about this kind of feline behaviour, of course; they are just far more sensitive to vibrations than we are.

People with psychic powers often claim to have telepathic 'conversations' with cats. They believe that an intuitive bond of love between owners and their cats creates a sense of 'being', of identity within the animal, thereby promoting their spiritual evolution.

Some Hindu gurus even say that by loving animals we give them the chance to take human form in future reincarnations. Although such ideas are not 'scientific', I am not inclined to scoff. For Christians who believe, as millions do, both in the existence of the soul and in the scientific principles of Darwinian evolution, it would seem logical to go on to accept that animals, cats in this case, also have souls, albeit at a different stage of spiritual evolution in comparison to us.

Mood detectors

It is commonly said that cats recognize and react appropriately to people who either love them or hate them. My cats are expert at this kind of instant diagnosis. Is this extra-sensory perception or, perhaps more likely, their fine senses of vision and hearing picking up subtle features of body language and tone of voice? From time to time you may have visitors over whom your cat fawns and makes the greatest of fuss, and some of these visitors will say 'How strange! I really don't like cats, you know, but they always come to me.' The explanation? The wicked, wayward sense of humour of some cats, I suggest.

Over the many years that I have treated big cats, I have become convinced that they are adept at detecting my mood. When I arrive at their quarters in an optimistic, cheerful frame of mind, they treat me completely differently from occasions when I am rather down, doubtful or preoccupied. It may be my voice and the general way I carry myself. If I am relaxed, they are amenable; however, if I am tense, they are more aggressive and crotchety.

We know that the chemical make-up of our perspiration changes according to our mental state. With their heightened sense of smell, do cats detect our mood in this way? It can certainly spot the change in the odour of our sweat if we are frightened. But could it be more than just their acute senses? Can they 'read' me in some special, secret way of which we know nothing? Certainly cats think in these situations and are from being 'mere machines' as St Thomas Aquinas so erroneously described non-human animals.

As for anecdotes of cats becoming disturbed when in the presence of owners discussing with vets their pet's imminent euthanasia, I have never witnessed such a display, but I cannot categorically deny that it is possible. It is an undoubted fact that cats look on vets, in the home or the surgery, with a particularly jaundiced eye. They spot syringes and needles being waved about and frequently proceed to make their feelings unmistakably felt, though I doubt they can understand words and phrases like 'euthanaze', 'put to sleep' or 'unlikely to recover'. However, again, they may very well be responding to the despondent, often distressed, tones and demeanour of a long-loving owner.

Homing devices

Another curious phenomenon occasionally seen in cats is their ability to travel long distances to find their home. One very long journey by a cat in search of its human associates was of 950 miles from Boston to Chicago, but the

Celestial navigation

Modern research suggests that the key to cat travel of this sort lies in celestial navigation similar to that employed by migrating birds. It works something like this: during the months or years that the cat was living in the original home, his brain registered the angle of the sun at certain times of day. (It is possible that the position of stars at night might also be registered.) How does the cat tell what time it is without wearing a watch? Most animals, we believe, possess internal biological clocks. Certainly man and the higher mammals have them. They have been located in lowly creatures like cockroaches, too.

Now suppose the cat is uprooted to a new home where the sun's angle at a certain time is slightly different. If it wants to put it right, the cat must begin by trial and error. In one direction, it finds that the angle gets worse. The cat tries another; the angle improves. That must be the direction to go. All this is a subconscious activity, of course, but, gradually, in trying to get the sun into the right spot at the right time, Puss finds himself in a neighbourhood where sights, smells and sounds are familiar. From then on it is plain sailing. So next time you see your cat stretching on the garden wall, remember – maybe he is just checking that the house has not moved!

record for determined return to a beloved home is held by a family pet in Oklahoma that was given to friends in California. Upon arrival, the cat, clearly unimpressed by the delights of tinsel town and Malibu, promptly set out on a walk of some 1,400 miles back to its original owners. It took fourteen months to complete, but the cat was positively identified on arrival by X-rays that confirmed the presence of an old hip deformity. How do they do it?

Most cats that are taken along when the family move house raise no objection and quickly set about staking out their new territory and arm-wrestling any felines on adjoining properties. Some, however, attached to the old homestead with its familiar hideaways, birds' nests, loose dustbin lids, dopier-than-average rodents and promiscuous members of the opposite sex, will have none of it and set out for their native land even before the estate agent has handed over the keys.

The ability to make for home does not work if the family move house, leaving their cat behind. It is not possible to track them down in a new residence if Puss has never visited it. It only happens if the family home stays put and the cat is hauled off to the back of beyond in a furniture lorry, cat-snatcher's van or similar vehicle. Freed, one hopes, at the end of the journey, the cat has a chance of plotting its route back to its own back yard.

Having said that, how can we explain that, when Shakespeare's friend, the Earl of Southampton, was imprisoned in the Tower of London, his black and white cat somehow discovered where he was being held, sought out the right cell, and entered by shinning down the chimney? A contemporary painting shows them doing 'porridge' together. That was a very clever, and thinking, cat.

The intelligence of the cat

'The cleverest puss pats the door handle, looks appealingly at the nearest human and goes 'waaah'. It works every time. I'm afraid a seven-month-old baby wouldn't do very well in this test.'

This answer was sent to *The Guardian* newspaper concerning a question posed by a reader: 'Which is more intelligent, my seven-month-old baby or my seven-year-old cat?' How intelligent is your cat? Is it possible even to talk about and compare the intelligence of other species that have totally different lifestyles from ourselves and with which we can barely communicate? There is much heated debate among psychologists dealing with just one animal species, *Homo sapiens*, as to whether intelligence tests are reliable when applied to people of different races and cultures. We have no good method of objectively comparing intelligence in non-human species.

The yardstick most commonly used to measure intelligence in animals is to compare brain weight with the length of the spinal cord. This ratio, which represents how much grey matter is controlling how much body, has the advantage of being an objective assessment, and should be bigger in more intelligent species. A human gives a ratio of 50:1, the marmoset monkey 18:1 and the cat 4:1; make of that what you will.

Nevertheless, it is perfectly evident, when using the word as commonly understood, that the cat is a very intelligent being. Solitary, self-reliant hunters tend to be. Their constructive use of their five, maybe six, senses is part and parcel of their intelligence. We have seen that in the way cats can locate prey at night and find their way home, sometimes over amazingly long distances.

How cats learn

We know cats learn well, both by experience and from instinct, and have well-developed long-term and short-term memory. Most domestic cats learn such useful knacks as tapping on window panes to gain entrance, opening a door by jumping for the handle, finding their way home or coming to the call of a familiar voice.

The first two to eight weeks of life is the critical learning period for cats. During this time they bond with their fellows and experience interaction with humans. Feral cats carry their basic mistrust of people throughout their lives if they are not exposed to humans during this time.

Cats and dogs learn in the same way but have different learning priorities. Dogs, for instance, quickly learn how to dig holes in snow to gain shelter. Cats don't; they have never needed to. On the other hand, cats cover up their deposits of urine and faeces; dogs don't.

Much of feline learning is achieved by observation – how drawers can be opened, how waste paper baskets can neatly be flicked over and how my gathering up the old newspapers in the morning to be put in the recycling bin means that the front door will presently be opened, so let's gather there to have a look outside!

Can cats be trained?

Domestic cats can be trained although it is a more difficult process than with dogs, horses or dolphins. However, I have worked with the famous white Arthur on the television commercials for the cat food which is named after him – he is a highly trained and accomplished performer whose speciality is using his paw as a spoon.

If you are patient, you can train your cat using a combination of rewards together with a system of communication, such as a clicker, which gives what animal trainers call a bridging signal, to sit, lie down and even jump through a hoop. Training must be by reward; cats respond badly to coercion and show none of the eagerness to please that we see commonly in dogs. Despite a source of rewards in the form of tasty titbits, they will only cooperate if they feel in the mood. Cats cannot be bought – that is part of their magnificent independence.

Stimulating intelligence?

Some people believe that you can enhance a cat's creative abilities and stimulate its intelligence by playing with it using coloured balls and patterned building blocks, letting it 'paint' by dabbling in a palette of non-toxic watercolours and then stomping on paper, showing it coloured photographs and encouraging it to watch television, particularly nature programmes. (Siegfried and Roy's white tigers in Las Vegas are provided with a television set in their luxurious housing.) I remain to be convinced.

Although, in cats, pattern and brightness are far more important than colour, they can be trained quite quickly to appreciate and respond to colour by using patterned colours and then gradually reducing the amount of patterning. All I can say is that I know cats that like to watch soccer on television; their eyes are attracted to the moving ball. As we know, cats' eyes are attuned to quickly moving objects. I doubt whether the animals gain anything else from watching a Beckham penalty.

Elderly cats

When they are old, there is a tendency for some cats to slow down, sleep more and become forgetful. Gradually, with the passage of time, as in us, dogs and most other animals, degenerative changes take place within the brain that result in a deterioration in their memory and learning abilities. A cat needs then to be handled with understanding, not scolded.

Cat chat: feline communication

Cats communicate – pass information – to others in a variety of different ways. These methods include the following: colour and pattern; body language; touch; scent; and vocalization.

Colour and pattern

Firstly, there are the permanent features of coat colour and patterning. The primary function of colouration is as camouflage, an aid to concealment. Desert species are lighter, often sandy coloured, while forest dwellers are darker. Patterns on the coat blend with the background, breaking up and hiding their outline against the patchwork of light and shade. Tigers in a zoo may look dramatic and very distinctive, but in their natural habitat their bold stripes and orange background are surprisingly effective in enabling them to merge with the forest undergrowth.

However, some pattern features act as signalling equipment. The black and white bands on the tip of a cheetah's tail form a 'follow me' banner, rather like the umbrella carried aloft by a guide for a party of Japanese tourists in the streets of London, when a mother is leading her cubs through long grass. The spots on the back surface of tigers' ears probably fulfil a similar function. Bobcats' tails are strikingly marked, and it seems likely that, by moving them about, the animals use them as a form of semaphore signalling. We do not yet understand the messages transmitted by bobcats in this way nor those of the caracal lynxes that apparently carry on conversations by twitching their black, tufted ears at one another.

The facial markings of felines serve to emphasize expressions formed by the mouth, eyes and ears, particularly those used to register a threatening attitude. Body markings too can accentuate signals sent by posture, such as threats of offence or defence. Whether or not coat patterns, which in some species such as the tiger are slightly different in each individual, might also be used by their fellows to recognize them, we do not know, but it is a distinct possibility.

Domestic cats obviously come in an amazing range of coat colours and patterns, mainly as a result of years of artificial selection by breeders, but with some of the original features of their wild forefathers in evidence. These include the tabby pattern of the African wild cat and the dark facial lines of many existing wild felines, including the lynx and the leopard cat.

The function of coat designs in pet cats is mainly to please owners' aesthetics, but the ancient usage of patterning as hunter's camouflage will still come in handy when Tom is out rabbiting in the local meadows. Facial, body and tail markings of domestic cats continue to give dramatic force to angry grimaces and postures of the body, and cats can undoubtedly recognize one another visually, but beyond that, there is seemingly little or no other use for coat colour and design in communication.

Body language

> *Then imitate the action of the tiger,*
> *Stiffen the sinews, summon up the blood....*
> *Now set the teeth and stretch the nostril wide,*
> *Hold hard the breath and bend up every spirit*
> *To his full height.*

So, brilliantly, did Shakespeare's Henry V advise his troops on the body language of the big cat. Body language is highly important to, and widely employed by, our domestic cats. An animal's mood and intentions are reflected in its carriage. A threat, whether offensive or defensive, is signalled visually in three main ways: by displaying the weaponry, usually teeth; by creating an illusion of increase in one's size; and by adopting some abrupt and startling change in appearance, such as erection of hair, flattening the back of ears, etc.

In an aggressive pose, ready to strike any second at an adversary, the cat has its ears pricked but laid back, eye pupils closed to slits, whiskers bristling forwards, mouth wide with lips curled back into a snarl and tail carried low, bristling and swishing from side to side. The body fur is smooth and the cat makes low growling and spitting noises. Like the grimaces and body poses of Maori warriors, all this is, hopefully, to unnerve the opponent, but also prepares the cat itself for the launch of the adrenalin-fuelled first strike.

A defensive cat that wants to signal its determination to give as good as it gets, stands with its back and tail arched, fur bristling, and its body turned at an angle to the aggressor. This is again, hopefully, to make it look bigger and less of a pushover. The pupils are wide open, the ears flattened and the mouth open with teeth displayed. ('See! I've got some handy gnashers, too!') This cat also makes hissing and spitting noises.

A brave cat

Among intelligent cats, one stands out. He was Simon, the only cat (so far) to receive the animal equivalent of the Victoria Cross, the Dickin Medal of the PDSA. Simon was a stray 'gangly green-eyed black-and-white tom cat' adopted in Hong Kong by the crew of HMS Amethyst, a Royal Navy convoy escort sloop in 1948. Like other Navy cats working as pest-controllers and companions, oblivious to the often noisy bustle around them, with queens known to produce healthy litters of kittens even under shellfire, Simon was a popular crew member. He stayed on board after the end of World War II, catching on average one rat per day and entertaining the officers' mess by party tricks, such as fishing ice cubes out of the water jug.

In 1949, Amethyst was at the centre of a notorious incident in China's Yangtse River where it was assisting Nationalist forces fighting Mao Tse Tung's communists. The ship came under heavy fire with great loss of life. Simon, who was sleeping in the captain's bunk, was blown out of his bed, knocked unconscious and suffered multiple shrapnel injuries. His whiskers were burnt off, his body fur singed and there were bleeding gashes on his back and legs. The sailors who, even at the height of the battle, tended his wounds did not expect him to survive. But he did! With the ventilation system out of action, the air on board was unbearably hot and, disturbed by the shelling, rats galore had invaded the ship's food stores and were even nibbling at sailors' toes as they tried to rest. Simon shrugged off his war wounds and at once set about tackling the rodent plague with great success. Perhaps more importantly, he was frequently to be found giving comfort to his shipmates, particularly the sick and injured ones. His unflappable nature and unfailing friendliness throughout were recognized by the Navy as a great help in boosting morale.

Simon died in quarantine at the early age of four years, almost a month after returning home to Plymouth. Crew members who visited him in quarantine were convinced he died of a broken heart, imagining his beloved shipmates had abandoned him. This brave cat was buried in a tiny coffin draped with a Union Jack and with full Naval honours at the PDSA pet cemetery in Ilford some days later.

When a cat is in a submissive, pacific mood, hoping to avoid conflict, it signals its benign intentions by cringing low to the ground with flattened whiskers and ears and a mouth which may be open and silent or half open and emitting a plaintive distress call.

Then, of course, there is the optimistic, imploring posture of the importuning cat that, politely but insistently, craves a favour, usually food and sometimes for a door to be opened, from its owner. Tail up and often moving languidly, head raised, ears pricked, eyes wide, alert and gazing intently at the object of its desire, the supplicant tries to look utterly charming. It usually succeeds.

Touch

Another means of feline communication is through touch. They do this by rubbing noses and pressing their bodies against or grooming others. Cats also rub against us in the most delightfully sensuous way, grooming and bumping with their foreheads any human who has gained their favour. These acts communicate affection and contentment and act to reinforce bonding with other individuals. My cats, no doubt like yours, also employ these touch signals when they want something from me.

Scratching, particularly of trees, is not done principally, as commonly supposed, just to sharpen the nails. The visible scratch marks, together with the scent deposited by the feet and rubbing with the body, serve to send messages to other cats regarding ownership of property and territorial boundaries. Wild cats, such as the leopard and African and European wild cats, also commonly engage in tree scratch communication, but tigers and pumas far less.

Scent

Sebaceous glands in a cat's skin, which elsewhere on the body produce the oil needed to keep the coat hairs glossy and in good condition, are modified in certain places, such as the chin and at the root of the tail, to secrete substances that give information. The sniffing cat's sensitive nostrils detect changes that take place in these chemicals as scent 'language'. Urine and faecal deposits also carry scent messages. Much up-to-the-minute information is exchanged in this way. Sniffing at the bottom, done on a regular, at least daily, basis surely cannot just be for recognition (sniff, sniff – oh, hello, Muffin, it's you!), particularly in a long-established houseful of cats. I believe things like mood and sexual status are communicated.

With urine traces it seems likely that cats can identify the individual cat that left them and, because the odour changes with time, when he or she last passed by. We mentioned the phenomenon of flehmen earlier (see page 24). It may well play a part in analyzing such 'messages'.

Scent marks are not randomly deposited but usually left at specific, meaningful places, such as entrances to the home or nesting place, on much-frequented pathways, particularly at crossing points, and at territorial boundaries. What is more, cats feel it is important to keep their scent markers fresh, so they renew them from time to time. Big cats do the same thing. George Adamson of *Born Free* fame once had a lion which, when riding home on the roof of his Land Rover, would insist on being allowed to get down and refresh the scent at every routine marking point along the way. (You don't argue with lions travelling on the roof of your car!)

The sense of smell is just one of the senses aroused when two cats meet. The complex process of ascertaining whether a new 'introduction' is friendly or not, involves all of the cat's methods of appraisal.

Vocalization

Cats, as we all know, can be highly vocal creatures, and do communicate with one another and humans by their voices. Each individual cat's voice is slightly different and distinguishable from any other, and they can recognize their friends and foes thereby. A cat's call can be used to locate a companion or to discourage the approach of a stranger. This is particularly true of the roars of lions and tigers and the grunting calls of leopards.

A queen uses her voice to sound the alarm for her kittens. If she growls, the youngsters respond instantly by scattering and vanishing. They hide under the nearest available cover, immobile, until the alarm is over. I mentioned earlier the function of purring as a 'dinner gong' for suckling kittens and later, as an aid to bonding between litter mates (see page 45). At a very early age, even before the eyes are open, kittens can show a defensive response to any disturbance by explosive hissing and spitting; this is more pronounced in wild feline species than domestic cats. Purrs, growls and screeches are also part of Pussy's courtship and mating rituals.

We all know that our pets have a range of different vocalizations: some angry, some plaintive, some fawning and obsequious. There does seem to be one feline 'word' for 'bird'; to me it sounds something like 'zsa zsa'. I have never heard it emitted except when a cat has just spotted a bird. Sitting in my office I frequently hear the 'zsa zsa' remark of one of my Birmans. Always when I look up, it is gazing eagerly at a pigeon perched on the chimney pot just outside the fanlight window.

Once some feline pundit told me that one can always make a friendly introduction to a strange cat by uttering the word 'miaow-PRP'. The cat would always respond civilly I was assured. I am afraid it has rarely worked. Perhaps my cat pronunciation is abysmal. I do have much more luck with tigers. Saying 'PRRRRRR-TCHA', rolling my tongue round the Rs and as loudly as possible, tigers will unfailingly come to me and answer 'PRRRRR-TCHA'. I have tried it in zoos and safari parks around the world with very pleasing results.

A scientist at Cornell University in America has some evidence that cats are gradually evolving into creatures that can more easily exploit us humans. As he, Dr Nicastro, puts it: 'Cats are domesticated animals that have learned what levers to push, what sounds to make to manage our emotions.' He believes that by artificial selection, owners choosing and breeding from those cats with the most pleasant voices, the animals are gradually getting better at getting what they want. Pleasant voices please people, and pleased people prefer to have cats with pleasant voices and also indulge their pets more. Some British scientists reject the idea of artificial selection causing evolutionary changes in cats' voices. Dr Bradshaw, an animal behaviourist at Bristol University, says that 'cats learn to miaow in ways that manipulate their owners. It's got nothing to do with evolution. It's simply a learned response.'

Perhaps the voice of the cat that we most like to hear is the greeting miaow when we come in through the front door. I hear it at around 4am each morning when Muffin jumps on the duvet. He will only say his 'good morning' miaow once, unless I am too ill mannered to respond. I always do, and then he settles down against me to nap until six. Very civilized.

Other means of communication

Are there any other ways in which a cat might be able to communicate? I have mentioned the possibility of telepathy for there is some evidence that some other species, certainly man and the dolphin, can 'mind read' in some way and at a distance. Perhaps cats also have the ability. There are many anecdotes suggesting it, and then there is the mystery of those silent cat conclaves! As Baudelaire wrote, 'Like those great sphinxes lounging through eternity in noble attitudes upon the desert sand, they gaze in curiosity at nothing, calm and wise.' Quite so.

Purring

One of the attractive features of *Felis catus* is its purring. It is a behaviour to be found across the feline species and has also been recorded in some non-feline carnivores, such as black bear cubs and the spotted hyaena, where the cubs do not purr but the nursing mothers do.

The principal function of purring in the domestic cat is as a bonding, reassuring, 'everything is OK' signal between mother and suckling kittens. Purring can be heard but, more importantly for young kittens, felt as vibrations. As they grow older and the kittens get out and about from their nesting place, their purring becomes a bonding signal between siblings. When the queen settles down to feed her litter, the first kitten to 'plug on' usually also begins to purr loudly. This acts as a 'dinner gong' summons to its littermates and ensures that no kitten misses a meal.

Purring is also part of the 'come hither' mating display of a queen on heat. The pleasant purring of a cat as it curls up on your lap or rubs against your legs is, again, an expression of 'all's well', relaxation and affection, though some purring leg-rubbers I know do it when importuning for food! And, as Beverley Nichols wrote in *Cat's A-Z*, 'nearly all will agree that the best purr of all, the purr that speaks most directly to the heart, is the first faint purr that comes from a frightened stray'.

Occasionally purring can be heard when cats are in extreme pain; what that signifies nobody knows. Thankfully I have heard purring in such circumstances only three times so far in my career, twice in domestic cat road accidents and once in a snow leopard with advanced cancer of the liver.

The mechanism that produces the purr was for long thought not to be a 'voice' coming from the larynx, but the sounds produced by the oscillation of blood carried by a large vein as it passes through, and is constricted by, the diaphragm, the muscle sheet separating chest from abdomen. Now researchers using small directional microphones have confirmed that the sound does indeed emanate from the area around the larynx or voice box.

The feline hairdresser

As compared with dogs, I am sure you will agree that cats are, not least in the sartorial sense of the word, smarter, always well turned out. Their crowning glory, like a woman's hair, is their fur, and it is usually tended, cleaned, tidied and adjusted so much better than that of your average tripe hound. Whoever heard of a cat, even a many times cross-bred, working class moggy, gleefully rolling, dog fashion, in cow muck? How often, though it can be done efficiently using baby shampoo, warm towels, a hair dryer and an iron will, is it absolutely essential to bath a cat?

Cats groom themselves thoroughly, regularly and often until, in some cases, they are old. Then, perhaps like some senior citizens who no longer care so much about snappy dressing or the need to impress their fellows, they begin to neglect themselves. It may, of course, also be part of a cat's old-age forgetfulness. Be that as it may, some old cats no longer groom sufficiently and their coat shows it, becoming unkempt, ragged or matted into cotts.

As the years slip by, production of oil by the cat's skin glands diminishes and the fur becomes less waterproof. Rain can penetrate the coat and, if it is matted, it may actually absorb the water, making the animal feel both cold and wet. No wonder many pensioner pussies abhor being outside on rainy days. Dense clumps of fur may also lead to the onset of skin disease. The

Cats' vocabulary

Cats do have a 'vocabulary' of miaows for use in different situations. There is, for example, one miaow for 'food, please' and another for 'open the door to the garden, please'. Each cat's vocabulary is personal. There is no common miaow word for 'food' or 'open door'. During its lifetime the cat learns the miaows that interest its owner and, more importantly, bring results! The cat can said to be thinking when it 'speaks' in this way. It is reacting to its internal senses which are registering its peckishness or need to go outside to urinate or meet the cat next door, but its choice of 'words', of the appropriate miaow, shows that it remembers what worked well in the past – truly the Thinking Cat.

humid, poorly ventilated microclimate beneath a clump is ideal for bacterial or fungal growth and an ideal refuge for skin parasites, such as fleas.

Regular grooming prevents matts

If an elderly cat begins to neglect its appearance it is up to the owner to redouble their efforts at grooming. Where matting and cotts have already built up, it often proves very difficult or even impossible to untangle them with brush and comb – they may well have to be cut off with scissors. This is a procedure fraught with risk. It is so very easy, when lifting up a clump of matted hair to cut it, also to raise up a tent of the cat's fine skin. Clip that and you have an instantaneous bleeding wound. I know, to my shame, I've done it. Real care is essential and in severe cases where the coat is in an advanced state of disorder, it is best for the vet to sort the cat out under heavy sedation but, as I have said before, regular grooming will avoid the necessity of ever having to take such measures.

Feline behaviour and food

If we could interpret feline language, I think we would surely find that cats' most popular topics of conversation are the trio of S-words – sleep, sex (at least among un-neutered inhabitants of Cat Town) and supper. Food is of immense importance, understandably, to cats and there are numerous examples of interesting behaviour associated with it.

We have seen how new-born kittens quickly begin suckling. It is surprising how rapidly they become able to distinguish between Mother's milk bar and imitations. At birth they will attempt to suck on anything that touches their mouths, thereby initiating a reflex response, but within a few days they will do this only when their lips come in contact with a real nipple. They are not like the young of other species, such as cattle or sheep, which tend to suck human fingers very readily. For the first three weeks of life, any nipple, even that of some other queen who is not lactating, will attract them.

Very young kittens spend up to eight hours a day in suckling, but this gradually diminishes to two to three hours a day by the time they reach three weeks of age. When weaning begins, the milk teeth are already fully in place. A youngster will begin trying solid food but spend only a few seconds at a time doing so. The queen later encourages her kittens to consume solids by spending time away from the nest and sitting or lying in postures where her nipples are not accessible to her young. As their tummies rumble, they are stimulated to investigate the food bowls instead.

Kittens weaned early, say at one month of age, learn to hunt more quickly than ones weaned four or five weeks later and the latter have less of a tendency to develop into hunter-killers. So, begin weaning late if you want to help the chances of survival of the songbirds in your garden or the baby rabbits in the meadow.

It is fascinating to watch kittens sampling food for the first time. Essentially they are inclined to try only what Mum is eating on the premise that if she likes it, then it's good enough for us. Gourmet preferences acquired by copying in this way as a kitten last for life and so, a liking for say, tinned tuna or Kat Weezul semi-moist morsels, can be passed down from generation to generation. Best to keep Mum off the titbits of caviar, oysters and smoked salmon at Christmas if she's rearing a litter, I suggest!

Fussy cats

One thing that has certainly changed as cats have become domesticated is their taste for food. Contact with humans has brought selective preference to the appetite and, yes, fussiness. There is no place for that in the life of the cat's wild relatives. Wild felines kill prey and feed as and when they can find it. Life is too hard to play the gourmet. A tiger doesn't go out on a Monday morning thinking, as his hunger gnaws, 'I fancy a bit of wild pig today for a change.' If the first prey animal he comes across is

Good hunters

So long as kittens have the opportunity to play hunting games with their mother, siblings or even just small inanimate objects, they can grow into efficient hunters as adults without ever having been exposed to prey animals in their youth. Kittens that have never hunted prey, or who have only learned to fish, experience no difficulty in catching mice. Conversely, however, cats that only had a mouse-hunting education as youngsters normally make a pig's ear of catching fish in later life. It seems that it is too late for them to learn how to cope with the watery medium.

a sambar deer he does not mutter to himself, 'Oh no, not sambar steak again!' and move on. He goes for it. Food is food; catch it while you can. There is one special exception to this. Tigers that are handicapped in some way through disease or accident (I recall a case where one tiger had a number of quills embedded painfully in his lips and paws after tangling unwisely with a porcupine) may become man-eaters. This is not, however, an example of selectivity on account of human meat being more toothsome to the big cat, but because people are easier to hunt down than fast-running deer or aggressive wild boar.

Pet pussies aren't like that at all as owners know to their cost, literally. Studies of domestic cats have shown that they prefer cat food to rats and mice, while feral domestic cats have a diet primarily of small rodents, but also take bigger mammals up to the size of a hare and birds as big as a hen. Insects and lizards, where abundant, are also eaten, as is, of course, garbage. Studies in California have shown that feral cats display seasonal variations in the type of prey eaten. For example, mice and voles form the biggest proportion of prey animals in January and February; the diet is largely of birds in June; and invertebrates, such as insects, tend not to be consumed from November through March. More rabbits are killed in April than any other month. Insect-eating mammals, such as shrews, are not very popular; they probably taste of ants' formic acid. If a cat does eat a shrew it normally vomits it up again fairly quickly, and when out hunting and killing shrews thereafter, will never again eat one. Birds, probably on account of those troublesome feathers, are often left uneaten.

Domestic cats seldom get the hang of plucking, unlike their South American relative, the ocelot, a bird-hunting specialist, which will dextrously strip all the feathers off even a small finch or sparrow, and while our moggies are often good at hooking fish out of water using their paws, they are averse to actually dunking their heads under the water surface in the way that the Fishing cat and Flat-headed cat do when looking for lunch.

Some individual domestic cats do show a talent for 'specialist' hunting, being particularly, and, to their owners exasperatingly, good at catching birds. Others are adept at nabbing insects. Thus has domestication led to the inevitable rise of the mighty pet food industry, and fussiness, much of it inherited as we saw earlier, is widespread.

In general, cats would rather eat food that is warm, at about 37°C, the temperature of a mammalian body. This preference harks back to its wild ancestors' usual practice of eating still steaming, fresh-killed meat, but may also be because warm food gives off more appetizing odours. A cat's acute sense of smell enables it to detect the earliest chemical changes in food as it begins to decompose. Meat that is 'going off', but looks and smells fine to human beings, will be rejected with a flick of a paw.

Discriminating cats

Cats also seem to be able to detect and thereby reject foods that are deficient in certain nutrients, such as Vitamin B1. It is thought that the Thinking Cat does this by remembering that after a day or two of eating the deficient foodstuff, which it can identify precisely by taste and smell, it did not feel as fit and up to the mark as usual. The clever animal makes the connection between one particular commodity and the effects it has on its body and, unlike you and me, who continue eating and drinking things that we know aren't good for us, it does something about it – deletes it from the daily menu. Very quickly, after just one meal of something that upsets their system, provoking diarrhoea or vomiting perhaps, cats can develop an aversion that can last for years. One of my Birmans tried fresh-boiled, high-quality coley fish as a kitten and promptly vomited. Ever since, a period of six years, although the dish is on the daily menu for the other cats in the house, she will not countenance it and steers clear.

Fruit and veg

I have already mentioned the fact that many pet cats have a liking for unusual, non-carnivore-type items of food, such as the occasional grape or, in the case of my Birmans, dry uncooked pasta. Wild felines are also known to snack from time to time on fruit and veg. The African serval goes further and often makes vegetables the main ingredients of its meals. Both lions and tigers will now and again eat grass and various fruits, the tigers of Manchuria being especially fond of cedar nuts which they eat shell and all. Jaguarondis and caracal lynxes love grapes and bananas. These hunter-killers obviously relish a variety of tastes and they are, again, acting very sensibly, for eating an occasional small amount of grass or other vegetable matter is also of value in helping the feline digestion. Pet cats probably benefit in the same way from eating a little grass and it is certainly not vain pampering for owners of permanently indoor cats to buy them the special cat grass boxes from pet shops.

Scratching displays

Unlike other carnivores, cats don't go in for burying food, making a cache for eating at a later date, although the puma is a possible exception to this. You will often see cats scratching the ground close to their food dish in a most determined manner. It appears to be a symbolic display of getting rid of any unwanted food remains – typical tidy cat behaviour, which in the wild would reduce the risk of unwanted visitors attracted by the smell of putrefaction. Domestic cats will do it after eating or when a particular dish is not to their liking at that precise moment. It is difficult, however, to explain why some cats do the scratching display before getting tucked in. Only one of my cats does this. As soon as she starts raking the floor near her dish, I know she is in a mood to eat. Perhaps scratching and food are linked in her mind, in some instinctive way, to some long-forgotten habit of her distant wild ancestors.

Feline obesity

Cats very sensibly seem to regulate their food intake and tend to overeat less than dogs. If they do occasionally binge, it is usually where a new kind of pet food is introduced and does not last for long. As a result, while about 30 per cent of the dog population (following human trends, I'm afraid) are obese, less than 10 per cent of cats could do with a spell at Weight Watchers. The typical domestic cat consumption of regular small amounts of food, a regime that improves digestion and the availability of important nutriments, is probably a major factor in the higher proportion of trim figures among felines, with consequent benefits to the health of the animals. Cats show a much lower incidence of ailments that can be associated with being overweight, such as arthritis, diabetes and heart problems.

The most obese cat I know of was a nine-year-old American tom called 'Spice' who weighed in at a gigantic 19.5 kg (43 lb). He had an excuse, however; it wasn't the effect of greedy gorging but because his thyroid gland was severely under-active. The ancient Greeks would have had a different explanation. They believed a cat's weight was controlled by the phases of the moon, increasing as it waxed and decreasing as it waned.

Stress-free, harmonious feline feeding

One final point about cats and feeding is linked to what we have learned about their hunting style and territorial tendencies. All cats, with the exception of the lions, are lone hunters. They go and get what they need by themselves and not as a pack or group. They also possess personal territories. It is therefore important that proper thought is given to the food and water arrangements in multi-cat households. It is not in a cat's nature to stand in line and queue for food or a drink of water. So if there is only one food dish and one water bowl, no matter how well filled they may be, for three cats, and if they are put down in the core territory of one individual, the result may be continual stress for the other cats, which are very likely to react by going off in search of less suitable sources of nourishment and drink. Most importantly, they may not be able to drink as much as they need.

It is essential to maintain a stress-free, harmonious household of cats by providing a sufficient number of food and water resources (and litter trays, for the same principles apply to them as we shall see) at various points around the house so that each cat can get what he wants, when he wants it, without fear of 'trespassing'.

Breed factors

Is there a connection between breed of cat and behaviour? It would certainly appear so with certain breed characteristics of temperament being inherited. Siamese, for example, are typical of cats that demand a particularly large amount of attention, usually by telling their owners so in a loud voice. At the risk of incensing certain breeders, for which I apologise in advance, here follows a list of some breeds grouped according to temperament. The more stars, the better the temperament and the friendlier and more suitable the cat is as a family pet.

★★★★★ *Five stars – Persian, Angora, Turkish Van, Manx, Scottish Fold, the three kinds of Rex, Birman, Ragdoll, Balinese, Somali, Tonkinese, Burmese, Shorthairs of various kinds, Egyptian Mau, Russian Blue, Ocicat, Bengal.*

★★★★ *Four stars – Maine Coon, Norwegian Forest, Siamese, Singapura, Abyssinian.*

★★★ *Three stars – Korat.*

The cat as individual

The cat. He walked by himself, and all places were alike to him.
Rudyard Kipling, *Just-So Stories*

Unthinking folk will sometimes say, 'It's only a cat', a pejorative remark usually implying that all cats are alike and of little account. They might as well say, but don't, 'People are people.' Cats, like human beings, are, each and every one, individuals and individual character is defined most clearly by behaviour.

The general behaviour of all members of a species, humans or cats, is broadly similar; the individuality comes in distinct aspects of behaviour. In essence, one cat is quite different from another. Individual behavioural characteristics of the cat are formed from a combination of influences – genetic, environmental and experiential, through learning and remembering.

Genetic factors

Genetically, a queen may pass down her, say, timid, shy nature to her kittens and there is evidence that forms of behaviour can be inherited from the father even though the kittens never come into contact with him after birth. Of course, the timid kittens I have just mentioned could also become that way, not through their genes, but by experience, copying the nervous and highly cautious way their mother does things. Genetic factors can have indirect effects on a cat's development.

Certain inherited coat patterns or eye colours may tend to be preferred by owners. This leads to the kittens being favoured with more attention, in the form of handling and stroking, for example, from those owners, and the youngsters, consequently, may grow up more human-friendly. It would then appear, but erroneously, as if, say, a particular set of colours and markings was genetically linked to friendliness.

Although early handling of kittens can result in their eyes opening at a younger age, a mixture of genetic and environmental factors are more important in affecting this. Among these are the sex of the kitten, the age of the mother, the amount of exposure to light and, most important of all, the father's input of genetic information.

Environmental factors

The environment, with its day-to-day experiences, obviously influences behaviour and, thereby, character. Competition for food in a multi-cat family can make some individuals dominant and others submissive, and events such as oestrus periods and the birth of kittens frequently cause dramatic, but usually temporary, alterations in behaviour. My Birman queen, Golda, an angelic, sweet-tempered creature normally, became a spitting, screeching, whirlwind of teeth and claws when another cat unwisely took a peek at her litter of kittens. Until they were weaned, she stalked our house like an Amazon.

2

A cat's life

The cat's life (or all nine of them if you prefer) revolves around its social relationships with its fellow felines and where sex and territory are of prime importance, together with varying degrees of dependence upon, and independence from, human beings.

Sex and the Thinking Cat

Cats multiply, given the chance, very easily. No more consideration goes into it than with many young humans. It is merely a matter of hormones, the chemical messengers that race around the body. Courtship, mating, pregnancy, birth and the raising of young are, however, a complex nexus of reactions to stimuli and intricate physiological mechanisms evolved over the millennia by the wild cats, large and small.

Sex, to the Thinking Cat, is primarily thought about, as in other areas of its life, reactively. Its senses, at mating time, are at their highest pitch and, as we saw earlier, they are known to be fully active while they sleep, and we also know that they dream. So, it cannot be denied that cats may well have erotic dreams, but without the ability to phrase feline sonnets in praise of the loved one as they slumber! I would give my eye teeth to know what a snow leopard dreams of, out there on the slopes of the Himalayas, with not quite the same backdrop as that of our neighbourhood top cat tom who sits on my garden fence in Richmond lustfully ogling, but to no avail, my two female, and neutered, Birmans.

Cross-breeding

This does sometimes occur between domestic cats and their wild relatives. The mysterious, very rarely seen Kellas cat of northern Scotland is probably a hybrid with domestic cat and Forest wild cat blood in its veins, and that delightful but very expensive breed of cat, the Bengal, was developed by crossing the Asian leopard cat with a domestic Tabby. In wild felines, cross-breeding between different species does not occur naturally but only as a result of man interfering. Zoos have engineered tiger-lion crosses, called tigons where the father is a tiger, and ligers where he is a lion. For many years I had the last tigon in Britain as my patient at the old Belle Vue Zoo in Manchester. Lion-leopard, jaguar-leopard and jaguar-leopard-lions have also been produced on occasion. There is no point or value in creating such hybrids except as publicity-creating menagerie attractions.

In many details, reproduction in the domestic cat differs from the basic system common to most mammals, some of which are surprisingly ingenious. Cats rival rabbits in the fecundity stakes. A queen is able to bear young throughout most of her adult life, and, with a relatively short pregnancy and average litter size of just under four, kittens can be brought forth in prodigious numbers. The largest litter size on record is of fourteen kittens born to a Persian queen in South Africa in 1974.

If the hormonal system is the master of feline (and human) sexual behaviour, the animal's acute senses are its henchmen. The thinking, entire tom is seduced, lured and controlled by his senses. The thinking queen uses her biochemically fuelled sexuality to beguile his vision, hearing, touch and smell. The rituals are the same in both well cared-for and feral domestic cats and very similar in most of the wild feline species. Domestic and feral cats have it comparatively easy when looking for a mate, but pity the poor solitary tiger when it goes in search of the opposite sex. It can have a range of as much as 1,200 square miles and has been known to walk 620 miles in twenty-two days.

The breeding season

A queen usually becomes sexually mature between seven and twelve months of age, although some Oriental cats precociously begin with oestrus (heat) cycles as early as four months. Toms mature sexually between ten and fourteen months of age. The queen's fertility period all depends on light, and her breeding season is linked to the length of the day. The cat's eyes automatically register the amount of light around and its duration, and pass on the information to the brain which, in turn, sends appropriate commands via hormones in the blood to the ovaries. A day length of twelve to fourteen hours is normally required to stimulate queens to 'cycle', and so in the United Kingdom the breeding season runs from about late January to September. There are exceptions and the exposure to high levels of artificial light in the home will complicate matters. I suppose that cats living up in the Arctic Circle must have extremely quiet sex lives during the long dark days of their winters.

Toms are sexually active all year round but have a sexy 'peak' in the spring and their sperm counts are higher during spring and summer than during the rest of the year. Queens come into heat for two to four days at approximately two-week intervals. This cycle is generally repeated two or three times in spring (mainly March and April) and again in summer (mainly June and July), with sometimes a third phase of activity in September. Again, as you might expect with cats, there are exceptions, with some queens doing their thing at any old time of year.

Courtship

As the queen comes into heat, her demeanour changes markedly under the powerful effects of the oestrogen chemicals released by her ovaries. She becomes more attentive and loving towards her owners, rubs more with her head and shoulder against people, other cats and objects, rolls on the floor more frequently and vocalizes. The plaintive calls she emits can be long, loud and frequent, particularly in Orientals, and, outdoors, can be heard by other cats at greater distances than normal.

The female becomes highly attractive to the male two or three days before she will allow mating. During this time any advances on the part of the tom, who often makes pleading calls, are repulsed by the queen spitting and striking out with her paws. He then withdraws a short distance and, after a few moments, tries his luck again.

When the female begins at last to relent, her behaviour changes. She is at first coquettish, approaching the male, purring, rolling seductively on the ground in front of him and even patting him gently with a paw whose claws are drawn in. At this stage, if the tom tries to mate, she will still reject him, moving away with almost an expression of indignation on her face. It's all an act, of course, which is designed to test the male's determination and persistence and, while all this unrequited flirting goes on, he may well be interrupted by other sex-hungry males who arrive on the scene and have to be driven off, sometimes by a bout of fighting.

A queen may refuse to mate with a tom which, in the past, has been guilty of infanticide: killing a litter of kittens, usually one that was sired by some other male. This kind of behaviour is also common in lions when new males drive out and replace existing pride males. With the cubs dead, the lionesses come into oestrus thus allowing the newcomer to replace existing progeny with his own, a bringing in of fresh genetic material with obvious biological advantages to the species. Domestic queens are not thought to return quickly into heat after the death of a litter. Nevertheless, any rejection of a tom with a record for kitten killing certainly seems to indicate that the female remembers, bears a grudge, and thinks.

Mating

At last the queen is in a mood to consent to mating. She places the front half of her body, legs extended, flat on the floor with her hind quarters raised, knees bent in a crouch, and tail to one side. The back is almost U-shaped as she begins slow treading movements with her hind feet. The male at this point is likely to make pleased chirping sounds.

The tom is now allowed to mount. He grips the fur of the back of her neck between his teeth and makes treading movements with his hind feet against her hindquarters. Penetration takes place, followed by up to twenty seconds of thrusting and then ejaculation. The cat penis is partly covered with backward-pointing horny spines. As the tom withdraws his penis, these spines seem to cause a stab of pain in the vagina which provokes a loud screech from the female and a growl from the male who jumps off and moves away. Frequently she will also strike out or twist round to spit angrily at the tom. The penis spines have an important function. The momentary pain stimulation sends a signal via nerves to the brain which immediately brings about ovulation, the shedding of eggs from the ovary.

After copulation the female will lick her genitalia and then indulge in more rolling and rubbing before mating again. In the course of repeated matings, the queen's sexual urges tend to increase, one might say become outrightly promiscuous, while those of the male gradually fade. As a result, she may accept several males during her heat period.

Pregnancy

If conception does not occur during mating, the queen comes into heat again around five weeks later. Where an egg or eggs have been fertilized, a pregnancy of between fifty-six and seventy-one, with an average of sixty-three, days begins. During pregnancy, physical and behavioural changes take place in the mother-to-be. She usually gains between one and two kilos (two and four pounds) in weight, develops a steadily enlarging abdomen, shows reddening of her nipples from about the third week of pregnancy and tends to become more 'maternal'.

Although the thoughtful owner will provide a snug kittening box in a warm and quiet spot, queens know best, and they will often elect to use some cupboard, open drawer or corner that they consider appropriate, shunning the lambskin-lined, heat pad-equipped, silk-draped feline maternity basket that came from Harrod's.

In feral cat society, a number of related females will frequently share a communal nesting place, sometimes even suckling each other's young. This system provides strength in numbers if rogue toms or any other troublemakers come a-visiting.

Birth

When the time comes, birth is usually a fairly brisk and undramatic event. In the first stage, which can last up to six hours, the uterine cervix opens and a bubble of placental membrane (the fluid-filled bag containing the kitten) enters it. Involuntary contractions of the uterine muscles begin to push the kitten towards the outside world. At this stage the queen will retire to her selected kittening place and may breathe more rapidly than normal, panting and purring, though not in pain.

The second stage of labour begins when the first kitten and its membranes enter the vagina, stimulating the mother to begin voluntary contractions of the abdominal muscles – so-called 'bearing-down'. At first this straining occurs every fifteen to thirty minutes, but then the interval between bouts of 'bearing-down' decreases to once every fifteen to thirty seconds and is accompanied by the emergence of a bubble of cloudy-coloured membrane from the vulva. The bubble increases in size and the first part of the kitten, usually the head, but sometimes the hind legs, can be seen within it. The queen continues pushing and the kitten is delivered. The second stage of labour normally lasts between ten and thirty minutes, certainly no

Bonding

While a queen will accept kittens that are not her own, and even those of another species, shortly after giving birth (cats have happily reared baby rats alongside their own offspring), once she has bonded, strange kittens are not readily accepted. The bond is not permanent; it clearly has to dissolve by the time the kittens gain their full independence. As soon as kittens are strong and active enough to leave the nest, usually at three to four weeks of age, the queen soon ceases to differentiate between her own and the young of others. Then 'wrong' kittens are frequently permitted to come suckling.

more than ninety minutes. Each kitten has its own set of membranes and placenta, except in the case of identical twins where a set may be shared.

The third stage of labour follows the birth of the kitten and consists of contractions of the uterine muscle under hormonal control, which expel the membranes and placenta. The interval between successive kitten births can vary from five minutes to two hours and some queens may deliver half the their litter and then rest for twelve to twenty-four hours before delivering the rest.

As soon as a kitten is born, the mother starts licking it vigorously to stimulate the first air-breathing respirations and circulation, peeling off the clinging remains of membrane, cleaning away the placental fluid and severing with her teeth the umbilical cord. She may eat the placenta and membranes, a sensible procedure in wild felines as it avoids soiling the nest and thereby attracting scavengers and predators. All this is done by instinct handed down through the long ages of cat evolution.

Kittenhood

The worth of a kitten from the night it is kittened until it shall open its eyes is a legal penny.
And from that time, until it shall kill mice, two legal pence.
And after it shall kill mice, four legal pence; and so it always remains.
The North Wales code of King Howel the Good c. AD 940

Immediately after being born, kittens begin seeking out maternal nipples to start suckling. Blind and deaf, capable only of squirming and wriggling, they use their senses of touch and smell, as well as their ability to register the warmth of objects, to do this, and each kitten in a litter quickly lays claim to its own nipple from which it sucks exclusively. Having ones own nipple is a good idea in a species like the domestic cat where lactation may continue for as long as five months.

During this time, teeth develop and any disputes over teat 'rights' could lead to damaging fights. Some wild cats, such as the cheetah, do not go in for teat ownership and cubs frequently change position when suckling, sometimes squabbling over the matter. As a kitten suckles, it purrs and exhibits the 'milk tread', alternating padding movements of the front paws pushing against the mother's breasts. This treading stimulates the queen to 'let down' her milk supply.

The queen instinctively knows how to look after her kittens, even if they are her first litter, during the vital next few days. A firm bond rapidly becomes established between mother and young in which the sense of smell plays an important role. Mothers and kittens recognize the particular individual odour of the secretions of each other's skin glands, particularly those situated on the head. The pleasurable rubbing of heads transfers the familiar scent.

Looking after the brood

A few days after the birth, a queen may decide to move her kittens to a new nest. Some will repeat this changing of address several times. Each kitten is grasped firmly by the scruff of its neck or round the chest and carried unceremoniously away. It is an instinctive act, also to be seen in wild felines, which moves babies away from the liquids associated with the birth process that might attract predators.

The queen pays a great deal of attention to her brood, licking them frequently to stimulate breathing and circulation, and toning the infant muscles. Kittens are at first incapable of passing motions or urine except in response to outside stimulation of the under-tail region. Bottoms are licked, both to clean and to teach them to defecate and urinate.

Communication between mother and young is mainly vocal at first with the queen producing a range of greeting, scolding, warning, soothing and

Learning by example

The transformation of the kitten from its blind and helpless newborn state to full independence takes about six months. During that time its physical and mental abilities mature steadily. The kitten's instinctive, inbuilt knowledge is progressively enhanced by a process of learning by observation, imitation and practice through play. A lone, artificially reared kitten with no role models to copy and emulate will never learn much of feline hunting skills. What is not learned during the formative first few weeks of life cannot be acquired later, and kittens that watch, and are in a very real sense taught by, their mothers, learn more quickly than they do by watching an unrelated adult.

'come-to-me' calls. Later, when the kittens have grown enough to go walking with Mum, visual signals, such as the queen's 'flag', her tail held vertically with the tip bent backwards, play a part.

Growing up

The kittens learn by watching their mother and other cats, but they also act by instinct. If they are disturbed while their eyes are still unopened, they will spit or hiss defensively. They generally only rest properly when together with their littermates, lying snugly, with the vibration of their own heartbeats reminiscent of what life was like in the warmth of their mother's womb. This instinctive habit not only serves to keep them warm *en masse* but also stops them becoming separated as a group.

Progress to independence moves quickly. Eyes begin to open at five to ten days of age and are fully open at eight to twenty days. At sixteen to twenty days, the kitten starts to crawl; at twenty-one to twenty-five days to toddle; and at one month to run. Weaning begins, with the first solid food taken, at three to four weeks, and by two months most kittens are fully weaned.

Educating the kittens

As is the case with us humans, there is no substitute for parental care, guidance and a good upbringing for young cats is, *pace* our political masters, education, education, education. It makes all the difference.

When kittens begin to eat solids, their mother and sometimes other females or, especially with Siamese, males, will bring food to them. Paternal care of this kind is also to be found in some wild species, such as the Bobcat and European wild cat. Male Canadian lynxes are also known to spend time with, groom and play with their young. Domestic cats may bring rodents or small birds for growing kittens. First a queen will eat a dead mouse that she has brought home in front of them. Later she will leave the dead animal for them to eat, and, finally, when they are two-and-a-half to three months of age, live prey is presented for them to kill – if they can. The queen watches carefully as they make their first attempts at emulating her, and, if the prey animal escapes, will catch it again and bring it back for them to try once more. Under her tuition they steadily learn and rehearse their killing techniques. Practising in this way alongside their littermates, the young cats are subjected to the stimulus of sibling competition making them ever more eager and urging them on to perfect the polished, lightning attack and lethal neck bite. Obviously all of this entails a great deal of thinking on the part of both queen and offspring.

Successful schooling in killing must be made early in life. If left too late, it becomes difficult, often to the point of impossibility. A kitten that has been deprived of maternal training of this sort by being taken from its mother too early generally grows up to be a non-killing adult. Of course, some owners welcome that.

Part of a family

A kitten packs a lot of learning and physical growth into half a year, equivalent to about ten years in the human life span, and, as with humans, a perfect feline upbringing can best be achieved by a family environment (normally a one-parent family in the case of the domestic cat). In raising a strong and sensible Thinking Cat, there is nothing to equal the natural milk and constant attention of the queen, the endless games and competition with siblings, and the opportunities to learn from and inwardly digest the example of mother and other sophisticated adults. It is the same with the young cubs of wild cats. Over the years, I have attended hundreds of young lions, tigers, leopards and other cat species in zoos and wildlife parks being reared by humans without the influence of feline kith and kin. Such animals are never quite as well adjusted as naturally reared ones and are often difficult to reintroduce into a naturally reared pride or group.

Sociable, playful kittens

In domestic cats, their relationship with humans seems to influence their rate of physical development. Kittens that are handled and stroked on a daily basis in their early weeks of life are younger, as compared to non-handled animals, when their eyes first open, and grow up to be more sociable with humans than cats who are not handled much before being obtained, as they frequently are, at seven or eight weeks of age.

Play is perhaps the most significant aspect of a young cat's development. Mammals are more playful than other animals and among mammals carnivores are undoubtedly the most playful – as hunters they need to play well to learn the techniques of successful survival. Because they have a longer period of 'childhood' than other mammals, excluding primates like us, before becoming independent and having to fend for themselves, they have more time to learn.

Stalking

This is introduced into games when kittens are about two months old. In order to keep things from becoming too realistic and perhaps getting nasty, kittens will often abort a play attack in its final phase to avoid contact with their 'prey'.

Playing for them is far more than just fun, something to pass the time between meals. It is schooling in serious adult activity. The games kittens play are theatre – imitations of what they will need to do in real life, but not carried out to the extent that might cause serious injury to or instil fear in their playmates. If a playful bite or scratch is a bit too powerful and hurts, the recipient will squeal and a lesson is learnt in being more gentle. Game playing with mother or siblings begins at about one month of age. Roughly three weeks later, the thrill of chasing one another is discovered, and play-fights, brimming with enthusiasm and accompanied by increasing amounts of vocalization and in which littermates constantly switch roles from attacker to defender, start at about the same time.

Learning through play

As well as exercising and strengthening the body, playing teaches such things as judgement of speed and distance, coordination of eye, ear and muscles, the timing of interception of moving targets and of striking with a paw. A young domestic cat living as a single pet learns less perfectly through playtime with its owner, and objects, such as balls of paper and autumn leaves blowing across the lawn, act as substitute targets. By practising 'hunting' a ball under the sideboard, hooking it out with a paw and then 'killing' it, a cat keeps the ancient essential skills in trim even though its tins of processed meat and dried pellets need no hunting or killing whatsoever. Many people, myself included, believe that such substitute hunting behaviour, particularly before being fed, makes a cat more eager to eat its rather monotonous diet.

Sometimes a kitten will be seen playing with imaginary objects, chasing after, striking at, things that are invisible to us. Is this some feline ability to visualize a target or prey animal when no material one is on hand for playing with, or do they really see things we cannot? Only the Thinking Cat can answer that. Play is also important as a kind of social 'glue', holding a group of young cats together and making them generally more amicable characters. Things change later.

Although adult cats will play with objects throughout their lives and sometimes indulge kittens in friendly games, social play involving other grown-up cats is uncommon and when it does occur, can lead to fighting. Play for them, after all, is now very close to the real, serious thing.

The neutered cat

The neutering of cats, castration under general anaesthetic of males and removing the ovaries (ovariectomy) of females, again under general anaesthetic, carries with it many benefits for animal and owner. Toms are far less inclined to wander off from home and get into scrapes, which can lead to serious injury and infection, and they can't get any of the local queens pregnant with unwanted kittens any more. Queens don't suffer the stress associated with heat periods and the pestering of toms and they do not continue to fill the world with more of the aforementioned unwanted kittens.

Un-neutered queens can have three litters of kittens a year for about twelve or thirteen years, although it is said that one tortoiseshell had her first, and last, kitten at the incredible age of twenty-eight. From about eight years of age, the size of litters drops, but it can be calculated easily that an unsupervised – let's be honest about it – uncared-for, un-neutered queen could give birth to hundreds of young over her lifetime. The record for kitten production is held by a queen from (where else!) Texas, who had her 420th kitten at the age of eighteen in 1952.

Advantages of neutering

The advantages of neutering are obvious. Toms give up their gallivanting, and their urine, so often sprayed around the home as territorial marking, loses most of its pungent macho odour. Queens aren't pestered by neighbourhood suitors who have the habit of leaving their urinary calling cards on your back doorstep. Oestrus periods, with all the restless caterwauling and attempts to go out cat clubbing, occur no more and, most important of all, the owner is not faced with home-finding for handfuls of young cats or, saddest of all, having them euthanazed.

Disadvantages of neutering

So, what are the disadvantages? Is neutering, as people sometimes say, 'cruel'? What changes in the neutered Thinking Cat? Neutering is certainly not cruel. The operations are carried out under full anaesthesia, are very safe, and are most unlikely to involve complications or be followed by medical after-effects. As the whole purpose of neutering, as far as the cat itself is concerned, is to lessen stress, harassment and the incidence of illness and injury, it is more than justified. It is most essentially humane and its value to the cat population as a whole is quite clear.

Some, but by no means the majority, of neutered cats tend to put on extra weight after the operation. Most neuters continue automatically to regulate their daily food intake, avoiding any tendency to obesity and not needing to be put on one of the slimming regimes now available.

Mentally, there is no doubt that the neutered Thinking Cat becomes somewhat more of a home-loving, calm and contented character, untroubled by the periodic swings in mood and behaviour that are fired by the powerful urgings of the sex hormones. Of course, its niche in the hierarchy of cat society, particularly as a tom, plummets, certainly in the neighbourhood, and also very often in multi-cat households. But he or she remains as intelligent, responsive and alert as ever. As we shall see, some males like, so it is recorded, eunuchs in the Turkish sultans' harems, may even retain a degree of sexual interest in the opposite sex.

It is worth noting that some cats which, instead of being neutered, receive progestagen type contraceptive/ anti sexual aggression medication for a long time can become rather lethargic and over weight, and occasionally lose hair and develop a 'pot belly'. Long-term use of this type of drug has also been implicated in triggering cases of diabetes, uterus inflammation and abnormality in function of the adrenal gland. I think these compounds are perfectly good and safe for the short term, but for a permanent effect on the cat, spaying or castration is much to be preferred.

The society cat

We will consider the cat's relationships within the family in the next chapter. First let us take a look at wider feline society. The social life of your domestic cat is as complex and busy as that of many a celebrity human. You and I know the layout of our neighbourhood like the back of our hand, know who lives where, does what, timetables of local transport, opening hours of shops and offices and what road, avenue or street is the most convenient route to the supermarket, doctor's surgery or church. So do cats.

By that I do not mean they appreciate that a number 190 bus goes to Clapham, that Dr Krippen starts consulting at 9am or that the owner of the posh manor house with pool and two gardeners is Alderman Kashpot, the slightly dodgy mayor. No, but cats look at the town plan, the streets, alleyways, houses, public buildings, plots of waste land and roundabouts as being not so much laid out as a human urban arrangement, but as a cat one. Theirs!

Like us, they aspire to property ownership, organize social clubs and even have a sort of driving licence! A cat map would show exactly the same features as one published by the Ordnance Survey but with different names for every detail, and the human electoral register would be replaced for them by a feline register, a list of cat inhabitants arranged, rather undemocratically, by social status. Dare I say it? Cat society is a bit reactionary, Victorian, snobbish and, yes, sexist. Pussy politics is of the right-wing variety.

Feline hierarchies

Now let us put their society under the microscope. Domestic cats go in for hierarchies. Theirs is not an egalitarian, but rather a quasi-fascist, regime. The cat population of each and every neighbourhood has its 'top cat' bosses, obedient lieutenants, grandes dames, up and coming 'Jack the Lads' (and Jills), 'ladies of easy virtue' and, of course, the hoi polloi, the plebs. As you might expect, the Mafiosi at the top lay claim to the biggest chunks of property and also demand the right to drive as fast as they like, when they like, down the middle of the road, ignoring traffic regulations, and hooting aggressively at drivers of cheaper cars. The underlings in general put up with this state of affairs, touch their forelocks – difficult for a shorthair, easier for a Norwegian Forest – to the big wigs and tend not to venture far from their dwelling-places.

How is this pecking order and property division of feline society organized? In essence, it all depends on sex. Basically, catdom is a matriarchy. On the top of the social pile sits the unneutered queen with the most kittens. After she is spayed, her position in society slumps. Males take their place in the community macho-style by using brawn over brain. The meanest, toughest toms, the Mike Tysons among cats, battle for power and prestige. Success in combat determines the tom's social niche.

The system is strict. Only occasionally does a cat lose its place by being vanquished by an up-and-coming young blade. Dominant toms do not necessarily acquire a large harem of queens, feline groupies. Queens appear to be more civilized than the males and do not automatically grant courtship rights to an all- conquering bruiser. Often queens will prefer suitors situated well down the pyramid of power – very fem lib and shades of Lady Chatterley. Top toms do rule the largest areas of territory, so it seems that in this respect, rather like the mediaeval barons of England, brute force rather than sexiness is more important.

At the bottom of the social ladder, on the moggies' Skid Row, are the neutered toms. As soon as an entire tom is castrated, he begins to lose his social position. After the operation, the level of the male sex hormone, testosterone, in his blood starts to decline and, as a consequence of this, the pungent masculine odour of his urine fades. The more it fades, the lower he slips down the hierarchy. It isn't that neutered toms cannot fight but rather that they lose their aggression. To his peers, the weakening scent of his urine is a powerful signal which, I suppose, is interpreted as the onset of effeminacy. In the macho world of tom cats you have to smell butch to be 'one of the boys'.

The importance of territory

In Cat Town, all cats, no matter how lowly in the hierarchy, own some territory. Females and neuters hold fairly small properties but will fight harder to defend them than any grandee tom with a vast estate. The problem for the big feline landowners, some of whom, in country areas with a sparse population of cats, may possess fifty acres or more, is that it is difficult to defend such extensive territory round the clock. No time to nap or lengthy mealtimes! In towns, properties may be as small as a backyard. Within the property the owner cat has his or her favourite places for sleeping, catching the sun and mounting guard.

Property is marked and identified as belonging to a particular owner in three ways. The boundaries may be sprayed with urine. (If a cat sprays you, take it without rancour, for he is regarding you favourably as a fixture in his estate!) A second method is scratching, particularly on wood, leaving visible and scent marks. Another way of marking ownership by odour is rubbing a solid object with the head, an act that transfers scent from sebaceous glands in the skin.

If you move house you can help your cat to obtain its own territory by discouraging visiting cats and breaking up fights. Eventually the local feline fraternity will yield up to the newcomer a piece of land of a size considered by them as being appropriate to your cat's agreed standing in their society.

The social whirl

Outside the private pussy properties there is common land organized on a 'municipal' basis. There are hunting grounds and meeting places and also 'no cat's lands', such as gardens inhabited by dogs and generally to be avoided. Meeting grounds are used for what are best described as 'social clubs'. Toms and queens gather to sit in these places in peaceful groups with individuals three to twenty feet apart. What these assemblies are for we do not know. Although such a meeting may include the mating of a queen in heat, normally the gatherings have no sexual overtones, but they do seem to play an important part in the animals' social lives. Perhaps they just enjoy feelings of 'togetherness' or purely looking at one another. Could they perhaps be gossiping, chatting, exchanging news and information in some mysterious way, telepathically for instance? Certainly, the solitary cat kept permanently indoors and thereby avoiding fights, accidents and disease, is missing something in not being a club member. It may be one reason why such cats, lonely and bored, can turn to undesirable behaviour like chewing carpets and urinating in forbidden places.

The class system

But what about class distinction when travelling around the cat municipality? Imagine what it would be like if you could not go shopping down the High Street between 10 and 12 o'clock in the morning because Alderman Kashpot will be walking there between those hours and the thoroughfare must be free of commoners during his royal progress and if, in the afternoon while taking a stroll down Blossom Lane, you spy Lady Lampwick coming in the opposite direction, whereupon she immediately sets about you with her umbrella and berates you at the top of her voice for having the temerity just to be there! Break the conventions in correct society and you can expect trouble!

In Cat Town there is a formal network of walkways or roads that link all the pieces of common ground and which skirt privately owned feline territories and non-cat areas. Some pathways are for the sole use of a particular cat; others are communal. Yet others can be used by cat A at certain hours of the day and at others by cats B, C and so on. It is a system designed to avoid conflict. The cat 'roadways' have their traffic rules. For example, any cat travelling along a main pathway has automatic and undisputed right of way over any other cat, whatever its social standing, be it ever so lofty, approaching on an intersecting side path. Come to think of it, that is just the same regulation that human drivers have to obey. Once again we see how very sensible cats are.

Feral cats

The social arrangements of feral domestic cats, cats that were once pets but have returned to living rough, are somewhat different. Each feral group is composed usually of cats that are related and is only as big as can be supported by the food sources to be found in their area. The group acts very much as a cooperative with females helping one another to rear litters of kittens, and a number of resident group males. As well as the latter, wandering males from other groups will occasionally drop by to sneak a mating with a queen or two. This is beneficial in bringing new genetic 'blood' into the community.

Locking out cats at night

I am totally against the putting out and locking out of cats at night. Such inconsiderate and risky management of a pet is never permissible. The cat flap is the ideal solution for essentially indoor cats that go out for exercise and to perform their bodily functions. At home, my Birmans are free to go in and out, day and night, via the cat flap. 'Outdoors' for them is our back garden where the top of the fence is fitted with a 'collar' of inward leaning trellis and plastic mesh. They cannot leave the garden, but have everything they need within it – bushes, flower beds, lawn, furniture and shelter, as well as a resident or occasional population of hedgehogs, squirrels, newts, toads and birds to entertain them. The cats haven't needed 'de-fleaing' for years and, not making contact directly with any of the neighbourhood feline mafiosi, possess excellent health records.

A feral group is affectionate to fellow members but antagonistic towards outsider cats. They engage in bonding by much rubbing of heads and sides of the body against one another, thereby exchanging scent from the specialized glands of the skin. In this way, all the cats of a particular group acquire a common scent profile, enabling them instantly to recognize 'one of their own'. A cat from another colony does not possess the same, shared group scent, and so will be identified as an interloper and probably sent packing without delay.

Feline family life

It's time to consider the social life of the cat *en famille*, as a member of a group of one or more humans and perhaps other cats and different kinds of animal.

House cats

Some cats live permanently indoors and seem utterly happy to have their owner completely to themselves. Tilly, the stunningly attractive Devon Rex who shares a flat with my niece, is a prime example. Quite rightly, owners living in high-rise town apartments value having such a welcoming companion as joint occupant, but there is no question of the cat ever going outside. This is a distinct advantage in terms of health and safety, but may cause psychological problems. Some breeds, the Maine Coon and Russian Blue, for example, are not suited to a totally indoor life and need regular access of some kind to the great outdoors. (Russian Blues can often be trained to walk on a lead, if you start when they are young.) Particularly if the owner is out at work during the day, it may be kindest to have two rather than just one cat, although certain animals would seem to prefer their own company. Some cats, whether able to go out or not, prefer to live with a dog in the house rather than other felines.

'Indoor cats', like the Cat Town population described earlier, also have their personal territories – a particular corner of a room or a favourite arm chair. Where several cats live in a household, indoor property rights gradually merge until all the cats jointly possess the house (with you, of course!) and mutually defend it should any feline outsiders dare to trespass.

Introducing a new household member

The bringing of a new cat (or dog) or baby into the house often causes tensions to rise among the established feline family members. New cats must be introduced carefully and gradually, always under your supervision. Older cats normally tolerate the arrival of a kitten better than that of another adult. The youngster may exasperate its elders with its constant attempts to play, sometimes being admonished with a soft paw cuff round the ear as a consequence, but it will not be seen as a competitor, a rival for territory. Nevertheless, as is the case with human beings, old cats are less able to change their ways and their thinking than young ones and so are generally more disturbed and affronted, and for longer, by a newcomer. Younger cats compromise and come to a *modus vivendum* more easily. Some old cats prefer to have a dog around rather than tiresome, bothersome individuals of the same species.

Bringing an adult into a family with three or four fully integrated adult, but not old, cats can be difficult. You must be patient and not surprised if bad behaviour in the form of urinating on the carpet or scratching and chewing at soft furnishings occurs. You are being admonished. If an old cat, say a rescue case, is introduced into a family of old cats, things tend to settle down more easily and faster. These old timers want to doze and dream of the old days, not do battle. I will deal with changes in the social affairs of pensioner cats later in the book (see page 161).

Reacting to visitors

The attitude of the family cat to human visitors, particularly strangers, can range from an effusive welcome to a vanishing act at the moment the doorbell rings. Some cats, even though well brought up and never having been mistreated by anybody, seem to have a natural, inborn suspicion that Attila the Hun is at the gates. One of my five cats, all of which have been brought up in the same way, has always been like that. The bell causes him to race immediately at full tilt up to my office in the attic. Very gradually though (he is now six years old), he does seem to be getting better. This innate suspicion probably stems from the cat family's essential nature, that of the cautious, ambushing, wary predator, overlaid with many centuries of poor treatment, even persecution, at the hands of mankind. Helping to ensure that your cat is sociable with visitors should begin early on. When someone arrives, the cat, if present or when it timidly shows its face, should not be totally ignored but fussed over and gentled a bit, talked about briefly and generally admired, in short introduced as an esteemed member of the family. Unfortunately, some of the most antisocial cats are those that live alone with an elderly owner who seldom receives visitors. I recall so many times as a young vet on house visits, being badly scratched and bitten while fishing with one arm under the sideboard for a terrified cat that thought it was making one last, desperate stand.

Family hierarchies

Where there are a number of cats living within a family, the hierarchical system described for outdoor feline relationships normally exists. Most of these cats have been neutered and the matriarchy clearly exerts its influence. Top of the heap are the queens, then, usually come their offspring, females slightly higher up than males, and below them reside the neutered toms. In practice, all this means is that, for example, where communal feeding bowls are provided, precedence decides who eats first, and the top cats have first choice of favourite napping or lookout spots. It is all done much more politely and lower key, with seldom any overt unpleasantness, compared to life out there in Cat Town. Although Golda, my neutered queen, is the smallest of my five Birmans, she is definitely deferred to by all the others. Mitzi, her daughter, also a smallish individual, vocally scolds or whinges at the three males if they act in any way presumptuously. I often imagine that in her voice I can hear the words, 'Watch out! Just remember whose daughter I am, boy!'

For a group of family cats there do not seem to be any traffic regulations like those enforced in Cat Town, as they move about the house, and the gathering of all the house cats in the sitting room of an evening, when their humans are reading or watching television, is not the same as the conclave of outdoor cats which I mentioned. They are enjoying proximity to their human family, not, I suggest, communing with one another.

This interaction with people is one of the most significant aspects of a domestic cat's social life. For them, we provide shelter, food, care and protection, as well as loving contact. For their part, these small creatures give us enduring pleasure and loyal companionship, and their hyper-acute senses and reactively thinking brains can register our mood changes and state of mind. Innumerable folk can testify to cats having paid particular, caressing attention to them when ill or distressed. It is now common for these pets to be allowed to visit patients in hospital, contacts that have been shown to help speed convalescence. The physical act of stroking a cat is known to slow the heart rate and reduce the blood pressure of a person.

Grieving cats

When a cat died in ancient Egypt, it was mandatory for its owner to shave off his eyebrows to register grief. When one of a family of cats dies, it is not unusual for these thinking animals to show signs of grief. This can be especially marked in such breeds as the Siamese and Burmese which tend to bond very firmly with their friends during life.

They may search the house for the missing individual, cry out or call incessantly, seek even more attention and fondling than usual from their owners or even go off their food completely. This can go on for some days. Rarely, cats have been reported as pining to death after the loss of a companion, and grieving can be exhibited in multi-species households when a dog or, yes it has happened, even a pet rabbit passes away.

Coping with grief

To help alleviate cat grieving, the acquisition of a new cat or kitten is often recommended. It may well help but not necessarily. Older cats may find a bouncy, live-wire kitten something of a headache. Bringing in two kittens may be a better idea where feasible, as the pair can work off their energy on one another, don't bother the veteran puss too much, and yet create interest, giving him something to watch.

Of course, there are cases where the death of one cat in the family permits another one, usually lower down in the pecking order, to move up and enjoy the privileges of its now deceased better. No longer bullied, it can take that warm spot on the window ledge and feed first at the dish of fresh-cooked coley. Such cats can seem to bloom rather than grieve, and may, who knows, be quietly pleased at the demise.

The death of a long-loved owner often results in pronounced signs of grieving in a cat. Fripon, a French alley cat, was so distressed by the death of his mistress, that he followed her funeral cortege to the cemetery and visited her grave every day thereafter. Old animals generally seem to suffer most. The effect on the pet is compounded where it has to be taken to a new home or, worse, a rescue cattery. Such cats need a great deal of understanding, attention and affection if they are to return to happiness.

Anti-depressive medication can be used under veterinary supervision as an aid at these times, but I personally have not found it to be very effective or free of side effects in the feline species.

Guidelines for keeping indoor cats

There are some fundamental points about having a cat in the house.

1 *Handle your cat frequently, picking up an adult by putting one hand under the chest just behind the front legs, and the other under the 'bottom, tucking the tail in. Once up, let him sit in the crook of your arm with his forepaws on your shoulder or held in your other hand.*

2 *Handle kittens especially carefully, as their rib cages are very soft and they can easily bruise internally if roughly treated.*

3 *Try to avoid picking up cats by the scruff of their neck except for brief periods when grabbing uncooperative or agitated individuals or if a cat has suffered a bodily injury. Scruffing a cat by taking firm hold of the loose skin at the back of the neck doesn't hurt the animal but is a rather undignified procedure, and cats, of all animals, detest losing their dignity.*

4 *Train your cat to do basic things like using a litter tray and the cat flap (see page 155).*

5 *All cats should be taught to recognize their own name. Use it regularly, particularly at feeding times. They learn quickly.*

6 *Have regular set times for feeding and grooming.*

7 *A cat can be left alone in a house or apartment for as long as twenty-four hours provided that adequate food, water and litter are provided. If you are likely to be away from home for longer than a day, arrange for a neighbour to call in and replenish food, etc. at least once every twenty-four hours. Neighbours are preferable to catteries (there is less risk of picking up a disease and the animal is not wrenched away from familiar surrounding). If no neighbour is available, professional cat visitors or 'sitters' can be found through Yellow Pages or newspaper advertisements in most localities.*

8 *Do not allow the cat access to dangerous items, such as poisonous house plants (see page 179), chewable electric wires or aromatic oils in vaporizers (often toxic when licked or in contact with the cat's skin).*

The cat as family member

Many families could not imagine not having at least one cat as a fully paid-up member of the household. In exchange for food, shelter, warmth and being caressed, the animal gives companionship, pleasure, interest and, above all, affection. Beyond that, cats, and other pet animals, are known to enhance the physical and mental well-being of the elderly, speed recovery of the sick and injured, and benefit the social development of children.

The exact structure and strength of the bond between owners and cats depend on the physical environment they share, and the temperament and behaviour of both parties. It does, however, seem to be true that owners worry more about their cats and the animals' living conditions than cats worry about their owners.

Cats live with people in a wide variety of types of accommodation: some spacious with many rooms, more than one storey and access to the outdoors, while others are more confined, sharing small flats with little or no opportunity to go outside. Cats, as a whole, tolerate all these different dwellings with admirable equanimity although some breeds are more suited to being kept permanently indoors. The incidence of behavioural problems is higher in such indoor cats than those with access to a garden or back yard.

Living in a small space

The topography of the space available is important to a cat's thinking and quality of life where its domicile is, say, a one-bedroom apartment. Being a creature that needs to move in three dimensions, it should have places where it can perch, keep watch, nap or hide away at different levels, as well as boxes, a scratching post, and toys to interest and amuse it, and a window ledge from which it can look out at the world and its birds and other beasts. This is especially important if the Thinking Cat is left alone for much of the day, and helps, by keeping his mind stimulated, to prevent the onset of aberrations in behaviour. Leaving the television or radio on may also be of value in this respect.

Best of all for 'loners' in small premises is another cat. Starting off with two kittens, ideally littermates, is the easiest way of doing this, as the introduction of a new animal to a long-established resident can otherwise be difficult and will need much time before some level of harmonious co-existence can be achieved.

Feline family lifestyle

The individual temperament, including that part which it holds in common with the rest of its breed if it is a pedigree, largely determines the style of the cat's family life. Any behavioural problems that arise may be due to factors inherent in the feline way of looking at things, the conduct of the human family members, the physical family environment in general, or some combination of these. We shall explore these matters later (see page 90).

The ways of the pensioner cat

I grow old... I grow old...
I shall wear the bottoms of my trousers rolled.

So lamented T. S. Eliot's J. Alfred Prufrock. Cats don't wear trousers but they grow old and, like us, behave and think differently as the years take their toll. How old is an old cat? The best way to estimate the equivalent age of a cat in human terms is as follows: a one-year-old cat is equivalent to a human of sixteen years, and a two-year-old cat to someone of twenty-four years. After that, each year's increase in the age of a cat is equivalent to four human years. The table below gives some examples.

So, if your cat lives to be fifteen or sixteen, he has done well. Several more years, and it is remarkable. The oldest cat on record whose age was verifiable was 'Puss', a tabby in Devonshire, who died in 1939 aged thirty-six years and one day. That equates to an astounding 160 human years, not counting the one-day extra!

On average, cats live longer than dogs – the rewards of a less stressful, more responsible life perhaps? Indoor cats have a life expectancy of fourteen years, although only seventeen per cent of British cats are over ten years of age while, according to an American survey, that of feral cats and pets that are free to go out on the tiles every night, is only two years. Without doubt, the first year of a cat's life, when it is newly independent, sexually mature

Cat age	Human age
1 year	16 years
2 years	24 years
3 years	28 years
4 years	32 years
8 years	48 years
12 years	64 years
15 years	76 years
20 years	96 years

and having to learn how to deal with a range of everyday risks, such as dogs and motor vehicles, is the most hazardous.

Physical ageing

As with us, the cat changes physically and in the way it thinks as the years go by. Some of the physical changes either mask or, alternatively, come in the disguise of, mental decline. Old cats need special attention and understanding. After years of faithful companionship, it would be a churlish owner who did not give thought, and make allowances for, feline geriatrics. Before turning to the thinking of the old cat we should take a look at some of the physical consequences of having nine lives in one.

At first sight, there may be little visible change in a cat's physical appearance even up to eleven or twelve years of age – a little lightening of dark whiskers, greying round the muzzle and darkening of lighter parts of the coat maybe. The feline figure may become stockier or, perhaps more often, weight may be lost. Internally, however, things are changing very gradually; the ageing gene is inexorably having its way and the machinery of the body's organs is slowing down imperceptibly. Age changes can begin in some tissues, as we shall see, as early as three years of age, and certainly with the coming of 'middle age' at around seven years, the animal's internal systems will be in decline.

Hard of hearing

Apparent lack of attention and 'day-dreaming' in the older Thinking Cat is not an indication that he is 'losing his marbles' but is frequently due to the onset of deafness. As in human beings, age brings its toll upon the hearing of our pets. Their sensitivity to high notes reduces quite quickly over the years, often beginning to decline as early as three years of age and usually showing marked loss by the time the cat reaches four-and-a-half years. Senility and diseases of various kinds can result in a cat

Smell and taste

The senses of smell and taste grow duller with age. The number of taste buds in the mouth declines and so part of the pleasure in eating is lost. Some elderly cats have diminished appetites because of this.

becoming stone deaf. Ear infections, ear parasite build-up and blockage with wax generally respond well to prompt veterinary treatment. White cats, particularly ones with blue eyes, have a hereditary genetic fault in their make-up that causes shrivelling of the incredibly delicate inner ear structures. This type of deafness is never amenable to treatment.

Geriatric diet

Venerable cats frequently become rather thin due to changes occurring in the metabolic processes of the liver and the waste-discharging functions of the kidneys. Veterinary treatment can be effective but not a complete cure in such cases, particularly if there are other symptoms, and the administration of anabolic hormones may help the cat to put on some flesh.

Where appetite increases, more high-quality protein food should be provided in the form of fish, meat and poultry, along with a variety of vegetables and, if acceptable, fruit. You can increase the amount of food in each meal or, better still, increase the number of daily meals. A teaspoonful of lard mixed with the food each day is also very beneficial in thin old cats.

Age may bring fussiness and the increased intake of high-quality protein may result in bowel sluggishness and constipation, as in some old people. Oily fish, like tinned sardines or pilchards in tomato sauce, are popular with many veteran cats and improve bowel movement, but the basic fault in most cases is that, in providing rich and tasty morsels to the old-timer, owners do not give enough roughage, the stuff that gives healthy exercise to the intestines. Mineral oil mixed with the food can be used occasionally, but regular use of it is bad as it cuts down absorption of Vitamins A, D and E. Puss can perhaps be encouraged to take fibre in his food in the form of bran or crumbled toasted wholemeal bread. If not, try one of the bulk-acting granular laxatives made from certain plant seed husks and available from the pharmacist. Mixed with meat or fish, these are usually eaten by the cat. Always give more water or milk if it is demanded, as denying any increased thirst would be very dangerous.

Deafness generally arises gradually, if at all, and is well coped with by the cat. Owners should play their part in compensating for the loss of this sense. It is important to remember that a deaf cat cannot hear if you are doing such things as moving the furniture, vacuuming the carpet or bringing a strange dog into the room – these are all potential dangers in the immediate vicinity from which a cat with good hearing will quickly remove itself. Certainly deaf cats should not be permitted to wander about out of doors, unless they are supervised or in an enclosed yard or garden.

Failing eyesight

A cat's eyesight may also begin to fail as it grows older. Changes within the eyes, such as thickening and increased rigidity of the lenses, may merely lessen the animal's appreciation of sharp detail. If it could read, it would definitely need spectacles. The development of cataracts – blue-white opacities in part or all of a lens – may cause slight visual impairment or even complete blindness. Other causes of blindness in old cats include tumours and diseases of the retina.

Again, in such cases, owners can act positively to help their pet adjust to its handicap. If you have a blind cat, make sure that you keep its food dishes always in the same place, protect it from open fires and similar dangers, and try to avoid rearranging the furniture. Sight is more important to cats than to dogs in whom the sense of smell plays a more dominant role; nevertheless, many blind cats continue, with a thoughtful owner beside them, to lead happy and contented lives. I would never advise euthanasia of a pet in cases of blindness alone.

Metabolic changes

With the passing years, the cat's metabolism, the chemical processes that give life and vitality to each body cell, changes to a lower gear. The production of hormones is reduced, the circulation weakens, the immune system become less efficient and damaged body cells are repaired and replaced at a much slower rate. These various alterations affect all the feline organs in different ways.

The skin and coat

The ageing cat's skin cells begin to receive less oxygen and nutriments than before; the oil-producing sebaceous glands and hair follicles become sluggish; and the elasticity of the skin is diminished. These changes combine, leading to the coat becoming duller, less sleek and soft, and tending to matt more easily, particularly when senior cats become less fastidious in grooming themselves, and in very old individuals there may be increasing hair loss. When this happens, owners must be prepared to groom the cat more often. Skin injuries heal more slowly and are more readily infected, and the incidence of skin tumours, some benign, but others malignant, begins to climb.

Waterworks problems

There is much less heart and lung disease in the old cat than in humans or dogs, but diseases such as bronchitis, congestive heart disease and tumours do sometimes occur. Problems with the 'waterworks', the urinary system, are more frequent. The cat kidneys, which in the young animal can concentrate the urine much more efficiently than those of humans, thereby needing a far smaller quantity of water to carry the same proportion of waste products out of the body, begin to weaken. As a consequence, the more dilute urine must increase in volume in order to get rid of the same amount of daily waste. More volume of urine means urinating more frequently. In addition, weakening kidneys can be less efficient in filtering toxins and waste chemicals out of the blood; their build-up can lead to illness. Loss of muscle tone in the wall of the bladder can prohibit it from emptying completely each time the animal urinates and this, in turn, may lead on to infection in the form of cystitis.

More frequent urination, incomplete bladder emptying and the possible complication of recurrent or chronic cystitis explain why some old cats 'have accidents', not managing to reach the litter tray or cat flap to the garden in time. Breakdowns in house training like this are frequently the first signs of senility in the Thinking Cat, but, note, at their roots lie physical changes, not mental ones, and, as such, many cases can be treated successfully by the veterinary surgeon. The old tom or queen is not necessarily becoming 'dirty' or forgetful or mad any more than a similarly afflicted old person is.

The musculo-skeletal system
This undergoes its own time changes. The feline body muscles diminish in volume overall and lose tone, with less efficient circulation of blood in them than when young. As a result the cat, but usually not before entering its teenage years, becomes less agile and athletic, moves more slowly and tires more quickly after bursts of activity. Cats suffer less from arthritic and 'rheumatic' ailments than dogs, but age degeneration of their joints does sometimes happen, causing them to exhibit reduced fluidity of movement, stiffness and pain.

Mental changes
When we consider the behaviour, the thinking, the brain of the old cat, it is clear that some things that one might attribute to mental or psychological changes may not be so, but rather the effects of malfunction in one organ or another. An incontinent cat may simply have incompetent kidneys. A cat that begins to ignore the call of its owner may be becoming deaf. A cat that knocks over a vase of flowers may be losing its sight rather than being wilfully destructive. But, on the other hand…

Brain degeneration
The brain, and thereby the thinking, of the old cat is not immune to the general physical changes that are taking place within the ageing body. Altered circulation, chemical changes that cause the degeneration of tissues and, above all, the fundamental effect of age on the vitality of cells, most especially brain cells which, once dead and gone, cannot be replaced, as is the case in other tissues such as liver, skin and bone, by new ones – all these can markedly affect the brains of old cats (and humans and dogs and all other mammals).

With the steady loss of brain cells over the years, the brain of a fifteen- or sixteen-year-old cat weighs only about three-quarters of what it did when the animal reached sexual maturity.

It is thought now that a specific syndrome, Feline Cognitive Dysfunction, can occur in old cats in which areas of degeneration appear in the brain. In some ways similar to Alzheimer's Disease in man, this condition may result in disorientation, alterations in social interaction, sleep disturbances and loss of house training. The ability to learn and remember is reduced.

How does an old cat think?

Although we shall be considering the Thinking Cat's behaviour in detail later on, it is worthwhile here to look in particular at the old cat's way of thinking, of reacting to the world around him, as his days as champion mouser and roof-top Lothario become a distant memory. It is undoubtedly true that old cats, like us, become more conservative as Father Time stumbles on, and they are more reluctant to accept change or cope with new ideas. However, at the same time, they have that invaluable asset, experience, and many cats in their teens are quicker at learning about changes, for example, in the location of feeding bowls, than youngsters.

Encountering new things

Their reactions to the voices of other cats and their skills in using their bodies to achieve certain ends, like winkling their favourite ping-pong ball out of a closed drawer, remain undiminished. Older cats continue to remember, at least unless and until physical degenerative processes occur in their brains. It is new things that they find disconcerting. For instance, a young cat will adapt to the arrival of a dog or a baby in the family far more quickly than an old timer.

Taking life easy

By and large, of course, the old cat takes life more easily, relaxes more, does not get excited so easily as the senses dull, reactions slow down and lusts pall. He enjoys just watching young cats play rather than joining in, much like old folk do with their grandchildren in the park and, again, like those people who have retired and now busy themselves with their gardens and planning next year's cruise, the old cat very often becomes more affable, considerate and affectionate towards his human family.

Going AWOL

Old cats squabble less with their peers and will grumpily tolerate, but not do battle with, any pesky newcomer cat in their household. Many, who are utterly content with their home comforts, wander less, but there are some that, perhaps through forgetfulness, go AWOL more often. Such vagrants need to be closely supervised, and possibly confined, by their owners.

Extrovert or withdrawn?

There are cats that become irritable and curmudgeonly in their old age. Others, once cheerful and extrovert, turn into nervous, rather withdrawn individuals who are frightened of their own shadows. Both of these types need regular, caring attention from their owner. Affectionate handling, fussing over, gentle grooming and low-key involvement of the animal in the life of the family will usually achieve wonders.

As conservatives by nature, old cats don't approve of changes of territory. Rearranging the furniture, redecorating, or, worst of all, a change of home, can disturb them considerably. If these things have to be done, you must introduce the cat, with lots of fuss and attention, to the new sofa, room or house slowly and progressively over a period of time. A new room can be made more old cat friendly by putting a dish of the grumbling pet's favourite food down in it temporarily.

House-training problems

I mentioned house-training toilet problems earlier. Some may be appropriately alleviated by medical treatment, but many, due to incurable weakness of kidneys or bladder muscle or where brain change

Arthritic cats

Gradually developing irritability in old cats may be associated with osteo-arthritis. Having just begun with the same complaint in my knees, I fully sympathise and excuse such 'grumpy old men'. Fortunately, although as in humans, osteo-arthritis cannot be truly cured, only alleviated, the veterinary surgeon can treat the condition effectively with one of a range of cortisone or non-cortisone type medicines. It is important that owners should not medicate such cases themselves without veterinary advice. Aspirin, and some of the other drugs ('Oh, let's try giving Puss some of those pills that do Grandma's rheumatics the world of good!') that give relief in human beings, as well as many of the anti-inflammatory medications which are used to treat arthritis in other species, such as dogs and horses, are toxic for cats.

'forgetfulness' is involved, cannot. Cats that once went outside to urinate and pass motions can be provided with indoor litter trays. Litter trays should be moved closer to favourite sleeping spots so that the animal has less distance to go when 'caught short', but don't place a tray close to the food and water dishes. Pussies, being particular about such things, don't wish to dine in the lavatory any more than you do, and are likely to react to such close proximity of lunch and loo by going off and passing water in some other inappropriate spot in the house, the very thing you wanted to avoid!

Some cats, particularly toms, seem to lose their aim when urinating on their litter boxes later in life. When that happens, a covered litter box of a proprietary 'cat loo' type is the solution. Such kennel-type facilities are usually welcomed by cats of all ages. Pussies are particular and also love privacy. To sum up, however, old cats have far fewer behavioural problems than young or middle-aged ones.

Sleeping habits

Old cats tend to change their sleeping habits but their activity/rest patterns increasingly mirror those of their owners. They sleep more than in their youth, over half of them napping for up to 18 hours a day, but the old routine may change, with the duration of each sleep period becoming shorter, longer or variable in length, and an animal that was once a night-long snoozer may now become active throughout the hours of darkness or vice versa. The pattern tends to be broadly set according to the sleeping and waking habits of the humans in the household, taking into account when the house is quiet with people in bed or out at work, or noisy with the bustle of the kitchen and watching television. Some very old cats sleep less than they ever did – perhaps no more than six hours a day.

Many cats seem, as they become older, to need more reassuring love and attention during the night and resort to calling regularly, loudly and plaintively for their owners to provide it. Among humans it is young children who cry out for parental solace at night; among cats it is the pensioners.

Holding back the years

Is there anything that can be done to combat the effects of ageing in the cat? Unfortunately, no one has yet discovered the elixir of youth for cats – or human beings. Nevertheless, recent research into the nutritional requirements of cats (and dogs) suggests that giving the animals anti-oxidant chemicals in their food as well as ensuring that they are well supplemented with vitamins and trace element minerals from, at the least the time they reach middle age, can help to protect the body, including the brain, cells from ageing and strengthen the immune system. Some proprietary cat foods now contain anti-oxidants, and multi-vitamin/mineral preparations are easily obtained from the pet shop or veterinary clinic.

There are certain drugs that a veterinarian may prescribe to counteract some of the symptoms of old age. One of these is sulphadiazine, which is claimed to combat senility, lack of lustre and greying of hair, and general reduction in interest and vitality where such signs are due solely to old age. There is also a range of anabolic hormones that encourage tissue building, oppose wastage of bodily protein, speed the healing processes and generally increase appetite, alertness and activity. The vet must decide whether your cat is suitable for treatment with any of these compounds.

When the time comes

To love your cat and be a responsible owner necessitates taking the correct and proper decisions when a cat comes to the end of its life. Hopefully, as for you and me, there will be no need for assisted termination of life. Death must be dignified, painless and free of fear for our beloved pets.

Arranging a gentle end

So when should an owner seriously consider euthanasia of their cat? If the animal is in severe, intractable pain or, in the opinion of a veterinary surgeon, is most unlikely to survive, or is suffering from something that is a grave embarrassment to its natural functioning, such as paralysis of the hind legs or intractable loss of control of the bowels or bladder, the humane, responsible and loving decision of the cat's best friend is to arrange a gentle end to its life.

Up to fifty years ago, while I was still a student of veterinary medicine, euthanasia of pets was far from perfect. Dogs were often shot, frequently with a captive bolt pistol, and cats were dispatched by the injection of strychnine or cyanide or in one of the RSPCA's chloroform boxes. Now, thank God, it is totally different.

A cat is 'put to sleep', still a nice phrase, by being given an injection, an overdose, of pain-free anaesthetic, usually a barbiturate of the kind that is contained in human sleeping pills. To me, the ideal end for Man's best friend is to spare it even the possible distress of that final journey in the cat box to the vet's surgery. Sedative tablets can be obtained from your veterinary surgeon and can be given to the animal thirty minutes before transporting it, so that it is totally unaware of being taken away from its much loved, familiar home surroundings. After that, the injection of the euthanazing preparation, having arrived at the surgery, is no more intrusive than a booster vaccination.

And then… I have for long consoled myself with these comforting words of Pam Brown:

I lack all certainty
yet still I hope
that at the edge of death I'll see
a small cat racing from the dark
to welcome me.

Problem behaviour

Cats are complex, fascinating animals that, from time to time, can behave in strange and sometimes undesirable and worrying ways. A responsible, concerned owner needs to understand the possible causes of such aberrations should they occur and what remedial action to take in helping the pet to return to normality.

Mad cats

As we cannot communicate with them by means of human speech to any great extent, we do not know whether cats ever suffer from psychiatric illness. Having said that, there's Saddam, a 'gardening' tom living near me with a profound penchant for uprooting each and every newly planted bulb in the neighbourhood, who I would dearly like to see lying on the psychoanalyst's couch. However, certainly brain disease does occur in cats, though, thankfully, very infrequently.

Disease of the Thinking Cat's brain, which weighs around twenty-five grammes as compared to the human brain's 1,300 grammes, affects the control centre of the body and, depending upon those areas of it that are involved, can cause malfunction of the senses, breakdown in the system of commands to the animal's muscles or loss of consciousness, and always, of course, distortion of the animal's thinking. The cat's perception of, and reaction to the world about it, its fundamental thought processes, will clearly, to a greater or lesser degree, be in trouble. When owners first contact a vet at the first sign of neurological symptoms in their pet, they commonly begin by saying, 'My cat is behaving strangely.' Mad? I don't think so. Although we can know nothing about cat psychiatric matters, these animals certainly can develop psychological disorders.

Environmental and social factors

Changes in a cat's environment and social relationships frequently induce alterations in its behaviour. The arrival in the home of a new cat or,

Orphaned kittens

These can present important psychological disturbances. The importance of the queen in developing the young cat's mind as she rears it cannot be over-emphasised. Fathers in this species are no substitute, and if tragedy befalls the queen while or shortly after giving birth, the owner can face problems of various kinds with the orphaned litter. I shall deal with this in detail later in this chapter (see page 100).

sometimes, a human baby can trigger it. Some bereaved cats may look for more cuddling and fussing over, and become noticeably more sociable with both animals and people, while others appear confused and depressed. On rare occasions, a cat has literally pined away and died of grief even though given abundant loving attention and even tranquillizers by its owner. The well-known human anti-depressive medication Prozac is nowadays sometimes prescribed in such cases and, with careful professional supervision, can be of great value for cats and some other species. (My most recent use of Prozac was for a female bottle-nosed dolphin grieving over her stillborn calf.)

Fortunately, the depression and aberrant behaviour that occurs in some grieving cats, normally passes off in a matter of days or, at most, a very few weeks. Time heals. In looking after any cat that is suffering from stress or depression, it is highly beneficial for the animal to get plenty of exercise. Exercise stimulates the brain to produce the mood-enhancing chemical, serotonin, and so indoor cats in particular should be given a variety of things with which they can 'work out.' Nowadays there are plenty of advertisements on the internet for such items of cat furniture as cat trees, kitty gyms, sculpted trees, stackable pieces and tubular playgrounds. If pets are trained to walk on the lead, regular trips around the neighbourhood are even better.

Other relatively short-lasting incidents can alter a cat's behaviour. Violent thunderstorms, fireworks or other loud noises and alarums can frighten these sensitive creatures into urinating in unusual places, hiding away and generally acting out of the ordinary. For especially nervous individuals, Bonfire Night is often very stressful, particularly in towns, and it is therefore best to consult your veterinary surgeon about suitable tranquillizers for them, which can be given in advance. Nervous or not, all cats should, if possible, be kept indoors at such times.

Medical factors
A variety of medical conditions can target the feline brain, including infections of a viral or bacterial origin, hormonal disorders, tumours and poisons, and there are, in addition, a number of neurological ailments without a known cause. Injuries to the head, typically through car accidents, will also sometimes result in damage to the cat's brain.

Symptoms generally include one or several of the following: behavioural or personality changes, tremor, convulsions, rigidity of the limbs, loss of balance, staggering gait, muscle spasms, abnormal carriage of the head, blindness, depression, dementia and coma. Precise diagnosis and treatment, which is effective in well over half the cases occurring in cats, demand prompt professional attention, and may involve blood and spinal fluid analysis, radiography or ultrasound examination.

Viral causes

Among viral causes the most dreaded is rabies, fortunately absent from the United Kingdom and many countries in Europe. Presenting itself in one of two extreme forms, so called 'paralytic' and 'furious', rabies is a highly fatal infection which is almost always transmitted by the bite of an affected animal. There is no treatment. Probably the most frightening thing that I have ever seen was a poor North East China tiger that had become literally mad, maniacally attacking everything – animal, mineral or vegetable – that it came across.

Cases of rabies have been reported in other wild feline species, including the ocelot, bobcat and puma. The only reported case so far of rabies in a captive exotic cat was an ocelot, captured as an immature individual in the South American jungle, and subsequently, but obviously unsuccessfully, vaccinated against the disease. Nowadays, British domestic cats (and dogs) being taken abroad on the new Pet Passport system are protected against rabies by an effective up-to-date vaccine.

A disease called Congenital Cerebellar Hypoplasia may be associated with Feline Panleucopenia (Feline Enteritis), against which all kittens should be vaccinated between nine to twelve weeks of age and subsequently boosted as recommended by the vet.

Another fairly common viral disease of cats, Feline Infectious Peritonitis, will sometimes produce symptoms of brain inflammation – swaying, falling, circling, paralysis or alterations in behaviour.

Hormonal causes

Hormonal disturbances can cause pronounced changes in behaviour. An excessive number of, or much prolonged, oestrous periods with the attendant vocalisations and typical, sometimes exaggerated, signs of heat, can be due to cysts developing in the ovaries. Hypersexuality in the tom, manifested by even more of a tendency to aggression, territory marking, roaming and excitability, is caused by over-production of the male sex hormone, testosterone, or, in a smaller number of cases, by malfunction of the outer layers of the brain (the cerebral cortex).

The symptoms of an overactive thyroid gland (hyperthyroidism) can include increased appetite accompanied by weight loss, general weakness and restlessness. A cat with the 'opposite' condition, an underactive thyroid (hypothyroidism), may become lethargic with a noticeable increase in weight and loss of sexual libido.

Addison's Disease, an uncommon malady of cats which is associated with abnormality in parts of the adrenal glands, may present trembling and muscular weakness among a variety of other symptoms. Again, all these ailments need prompt attention and diagnosis by a veterinarian, but they can, in most cases, be treated successfully.

Brain diseases

Brain tumours of several types, both benign and malignant, sometimes develop within brain tissue. There may be a single primary tumour or a number of tumours, secondary to a cancerous growth elsewhere in the body. One of the commonest symptoms that I have seen in cats with such growths is a fairly sudden change in temperament and behaviour. An animal that normally was placid, even-tempered and affectionate becomes highly-strung, anti-social and aggressive, spitting malevolently and striking out both at other family cats and concerned owners.

Feline Spongiform Encephalopathy (FSE)

Among the brain diseases whose causes we do not yet fully understand, is Feline Spongiform Encephalopathy (FSE), the cat version of 'Mad Cow' disease (BSE) and vCJD (variant Creuztfeldt-Jacob Disease) of humans. In this condition, areas of brain damage are accompanied by the appearance of mysterious scraps of protein called prions. First symptoms, arriving after a long incubation period, may present themselves as wobbliness, stumbling, and postural difficulties, but owners should be aware that these signs are also among those produced more commonly by other, treatable afflictions such as Otitis Media (Middle Ear Disease).

FSE has so far only been reported in domestic cats in Great Britain and was first recognized in 1990. There have also been cases in non-domesticated cats including an ocelot, pumas and cheetahs, two of which my partner, Dr John Lewis, and I had as patients in the last days of Windsor Safari Park. It seems that the disease is linked to eating cow meat products, but no one proprietary brand of cat food has been implicated and it is possible, though unlikely, that other routes of infection, for example through the placenta to kittens in the womb, may exist. The number of cats affected by FSE in Britain is relatively small so far and the steps taken by the authorities to eradicate BSE in the meat chain in this country will equally well protect domestic cats from FSE in

Toxic substances

In and around every home there are a number of common substances that are toxic to cats and can induce symptoms of brain malfunction if licked, swallowed or, in some cases, merely touched. Among these are alphachloralose, thallium and zinc phosphide-containing rodenticides, metaldehyde-containing slug killers, phenolic chemicals (creosote, tar, pitch, Jeye's Fluid, carbolic drain disinfectants, etc.) which can poison not only by ingestion but also through contact with the skin, car antifreeze liquid (often readily lapped from puddles in the garage and, apparently, the commonest poison used by unscrupulous rival competitors at cat shows in the United States to nobble other folk's animals via their show cage water pots), strychnine-containing rodent and (illegal) bird poisons, the venom secreted by toad skin, wasp stings, and adder bite venom (which is seen from time to time in high summer, usually in cats living in the Yorkshire Dales, Dorset or the West Country).

While quick veterinary attention is, of course, essential in cases where poisoning is suspected to have occurred, it may be useful for owners to have information on the principal symptoms of some of these chemicals and the antidotes that can be used. Here is a list:

Alphachloralose rodenticides
Symptoms: *Staggering, low temperature, coma*
Treatment: *Emetics, Valium (if convulsions occur), warmth. No sedatives*

Antifreeze (ethylene glycol) fluid
Symptoms: *Depression, incoordination, convulsions, coma*
Treatment: *Alcohol (ethyl alcohol), sodium bicarbonate*

the future we believe. With 'Mad Cow Disease' turning up in the United States in late 2003, it is fervently to be hoped that cases of FSE in American cats do not follow.

I mentioned earlier the old age-related degeneration of brain tissue which is involved in the condition called Feline Cognitive Dysfunction. The symptoms of this, like forgetfulness and absent-mindedness, tend to come on gradually and, in some cases, may never be very distinct.

Snake venom
Symptoms: *Hyperexcitability, depression, tremors, staggering, dilated pupils, collapse*
Treatment: *Specific adder antivenin*

Toad venom
Symptoms: *Salivation, retching, convulsions, collapse*
Treatment: *Mouth wash, corticosteroids, barbiturate sedatives*

Strychnine
Symptoms: *Hyperexcitability, tremors, spasms, convulsions, salivation, vomiting*
Treatment: *Barbiturate sedatives*

Thallium rodenticides
Symptoms: *Salivation, vomiting, convulsions, pain, diarrhoea, laboured breathing, loss of hair, scaly skin*
Treatment: *Emetics, purgatives, Prussian Blue orally*

Zinc phosphide rodenticides
Symptoms: *Vomiting, abdominal pain, convulsions, depression, coma*
Treatment: *Stomach wash out*

Metaldehyde slug killers
Symptoms: *Hypersensitivity to light and to being touched, tremors, incoordination, salivation, convulsions, coma*
Treatment: *Sedatives*

Wasp stings
Symptoms: *Pain and other symptoms, depending on where stung and how many times. With multiple stings, vomiting, diarrhoea, collapse*
Treatment: *Antihistamines, corticosteroids*

A final word...

The important points to remember are that brain and nervous system aberrations can come in many guises, need veterinary diagnosis, often can be treated successfully and, most emphatically, do not mean that the cat is turning into a lunatic. Whatever the circumstance or condition that is troubling your cat, there is no substitute for liberal dosing with tender, loving care. Frequent attention, gentle handling, talking to it, providing a warm, comfortable bed and fresh, tasty, favourite foods – these are the things that help speed a return to normal (and for human beings in a similar position, come to think of it).

Over-grooming

Turning to the diametrically opposite kind of grooming cat to the neglectful geriatric, we must now consider the fanatical over-groomer, the cat that never gives up on its coat. The normal cat spends an impressive 30–40 per cent of its waking hours grooming itself. Over-grooming, which can go so far that fur is lost and bald patches appear, is a psychological condition of the type labelled as stereotypic or obsessive-compulsive. It belongs to the same group of abnormal behaviour patterns as the incessant to and fro pacing sometimes seen in zoo tigers.

Before deciding that any particular cat is an obsessive over-groomer, the vet will examine it to eliminate the possibility that an itchy skin, perhaps as a result of allergy to flea bite saliva or some other kind of irritating dermatitis, might lie at the root of the phenomenon. An obsessive-compulsive disorder like over-grooming is an abnormal, excessive, unnecessary, recurring behaviour over which the cat has no control. It does not seem able to decide when to start or stop it, but is simply driven to do it.

Causes of over-grooming

The problem can arise in the first place either from boredom or stress if the cat is anxious about or in conflict with some aspect of its environment. In an unknown percentage of cases, the anxiety of the cat is not induced by external events or circumstances but is internal, involved with chemical and electrical triggers in the brain. An owner can unwittingly reinforce the abnormal behaviour at first by giving treats or special attention, items that are interpreted by the cat as being rewards. Eventually the bizarre behaviour continues relentlessly even if the original source of motivation no longer exists.

Treating over-grooming

Mild over-grooming or any other type of obsessive behaviour need not be treated so long as there are no physical ill effects on the cat, and the owner is not disturbed by it. When treatment is deemed necessary, the owner can try to distract the cat in mid-performance, not at that time by giving a pleasant reward but by the use of, say, a sudden, sharp noise (a short blast from a police whistle, a loud clap of the hands, a gong, etc.) or a judicious squirt from a water pistol. Then, as soon as the animal is distracted, alternative behaviour should be stimulated with the owner lavishing attention, starting a game or providing a toy.

As we shall see, training some of the simple behaviours (see page 151) could also be a valuable option. For success, it is vital that both owner and cat recognize that the reward is not for doing the wrong thing but for *stopping* doing the wrong thing. Timing the reward until after the cue, sound or squirt, and the correct response, cessation of the behaviour, has been delivered by the cat, is the crucial item. Punishment that increases anxiety should *never* be used.

Naturally an effort must be made to identify the cause of the compulsion in the first place. Is there a new member of the household, perhaps a baby, or has someone left home? Is there a next-door cat trying to usurp territory and acting belligerently? Has the cat's favourite sleeping spot been disturbed by a source of noise like a re-positioned CD player or completely lost by re-arrangement of furniture? In a multi-cat household, particular attention should be paid to the social relationships between the various animals. Aggression can occur without obvious displays of animosity or antipathy. Threats can be made silently, by adopting a certain posture or provocatively using another cat's private territory for example.

It is important that, day by day, the cat receives steady attention, is handled and played with and has a variety of toys and devices to interest it and play with, as well as, crucially, a snug, peaceful place where it can rest.

If all else fails the vet might prescribe medication for the obsessive-compulsive patient. Drugs, such as Prozac and, particularly in the United States, clomipramine, administered for at least three months, have proved beneficial, but side effects can occur and little is known as yet about possible longterm effects.

Other obsessive-compulsive behaviours

These include the so-called 'twitchy cat disease' (feline hyperaesthesia) where the skin suddenly ripples and twitches. The cat may jump up and run to nowhere in particular and for no obvious reason, sometimes apparently hallucinating. I consider it very feasible that this latter type of behaviour originates inside the cat, as mentioned earlier, in the neuro-chemistry of the brain. Unfortunately, the animal cannot tell us what it 'sees' or what is the nature of its imagined anxiety or fear at such moments. The brain chemicals may conceivably create an effect similar to that experienced by a person on an LSD 'trip', but shorter lasting. As is the case in some human patients with related conditions, cats might be frightened but not know what they are frightened of.

An affected cat may also bite at its flanks, legs or tail. Some, but not all, cases of urine-spraying in undesirable places are also obsessive-compulsive, as can be persistent bouts of tail-chasing, repetitive bouts of vocalization, chewing or plucking out its own fur, bizarre appetite – eating such things as candle wax, coconut matting or plastic, for example – wool sucking, and wool and fabric chewing.

Fabric chewing is more commonly found in Oriental breeds, particularly

Wool sucking

Many years ago I was called to see a Burmese belonging to Dr Steptoe, the renowned Louise Brown 'test tube baby' fertility expert. The cat had brown wool trailing out of its mouth and also out of its anus. I soon realised that the string was extending right through the whole length of the gullet, stomach, small and large intestines. To pull one end would have caused fatal damage by making the bowels 'concertina' with the wool cutting into the delicate gut lining at several points. That cat had to have an immediate operation. The abdomen was opened and then incisions made at a number of places in the bowel wall so that the wool could be extracted in pieces.

Wild cats

The only condition in wild cats that might be considered an obsessive-compulsive behaviour, and which I have encountered, is so-called 'star-gazing' in tigers. Here the big cat stands transfixed, staring unblinking at the heavens for many minutes at a time. Once reasonably common, it is now come across far less often. Years ago it was attributed to congenital brain disorder or Vitamin A deficiency. I do not know, but it was certainly virtually impossible to treat.

Siamese and Burmese. The behaviour typically starts at between two and eight months of age. Many begin with wool before moving on to other fabrics. Balls of wool can be especially dangerous as the cat may start to swallow a string of the material and keep on swallowing! Wool sucking and also sucking the ears of siblings is frequently seen in orphan kittens. It is probably a throwback to the happy days of suckling now so abruptly terminated. Weaning a kitten too early may have a similar effect.

What causes this behaviour?

The causes of all these various forms of obsessive-compulsive behaviour are in general the same as those described for excessive grooming, the principal one being some form of stress, and both owner and vet will use the same methods in tackling the problems. Some experts suggest that cases of bizarre appetite can be alleviated by increasing the amount of fibre, such as bran in the diet or by giving the cat a gristly bone to chew on.

In some instances, overeating or underj188

eating are obsessive-compulsive disorders, but, as ever, these patients need veterinary examination to confirm that no physical medical explanation of them exists (diabetes, thyroid disease, etc.) before it can be assumed that they are psychological. It is so easy to be led astray; examples of physical disease mimicking psychological disorders include deafness and lead poisoning that can cause repetitive miaowing, and Vitamin B1 deficiency (caused by an all-fish diet) inducing fabric chewing.

If a cat's behaviour gets to the point where the owner feels they can no longer cope, it is advisable to consult an animal behaviourist, many of whom specialize in feline psychological matters, for further help. Fortunately, the only obsessions my Birmans have as yet manifested are with gently poached coley fillets and drinking water out of our flower vases. I suspect there is no cure.

Little orphan Kitty

There are still large numbers of orphan cats to be found. True, as a result of advances in veterinary medicine over the past twenty years, far fewer queens die during, or as a result of, having kittens, but folk still exist who, despicably, dump unwanted kittens alive in dustbins, hardly a kinder way of disposing of them than, equally despicably, by drowning.

Unlike the situation with human beings, orphan cats are those that have lost just one parent, and it is always their mother. Fathers have no role to play in bringing up kittens, with the minor occasional exceptions of food-bringing to weaning youngsters by Siamese toms and, so it is recorded, tigers. As is so often said and written, to the point of tedium, about human children, parental guidance, role models and the way kids are treated when in their formative years, are the major influences shaping adult character and behaviour. It is exactly the same for cats. A correctly brought-up kitten becomes a correctly behaving cat.

The worst situation is when a kitten is left to face the world alone, without any siblings. At least if it is one of a litter of orphans some of its social development can be catered for, and it will enjoy body warmth and companionship and learn the arts of cat play. Wherever possible, do try to keep a litter of orphans together. Only if a newborn kitten is seriously deformed, with cleft palate, an imperforate anus or hydrocephalus ('water on the brain'), for example, should it be euthanased humanely. Seek veterinary advice if the animal is at all physically 'odd' in any way.

Feeding orphans

Feeding an orphan kitten, either by foster mother or using one of the proprietary brands of powdered or liquid cat milk substitutes (specially formulated for cats and not the same as the products for human babies or puppies), is not difficult, but will take lots of your time over a period of a few weeks. Goat's milk is rather weaker than cat milk but has been used for short periods satisfactorily. Cow's milk can be used in an emergency and preferably only for a day or two, but has to be modified.

I suggest making up the following formula: two-thirds of a cup of whole cow's milk mixed with three raw egg yolks, one tablespoon corn oil and one drop of a human-type multivitamin liquid, such as Abidec. A newborn kitten will need to be fed ten times in every twenty-four-hour period.

If the kitten can receive at least a little of its mother's first milk (colostrum) within eight hours of its birth, this is invaluable, as it contains important disease antibodies that help protect the baby until it is old enough to be vaccinated. There is no substitute for it but, if a foster mother who is in the first day or two of lactating, is available, her milk may supply some antibodies. Tiny feeding bottles and teats can be obtained from pet shops or vets. There are other ways of hand-feeding kittens – by syringe, dropper or tube, for example – but these, along with all matters concerning the physical well-being and maintenance of your orphan, should be discussed with your vet. Local cat breeders are also excellent sources of advice and information.

Healthy development

My main concern here is, however, the mental health and development of the Thinking Kitten, and this warrants being given plenty of intelligent consideration. The thing that an orphan misses most, of course, is the care, attention and education afforded by a nursing queen. The care of the mother, involving the cleaning and grooming of her babies, is not just a matter of hygiene and tidiness; it creates unique psychological bonds. Suckling gives comfort and security as well as milk and, if no mother is around, some kittens will engage in sucking human fingers or their littermates' ears, tails or feet.

Human care can replace that of a queen but, if it is overdone, it may lead to the cat becoming too dependent, over-attached and excessively demanding later in life. Some individuals even end up dominating the household. To be most successful in establishing social relationships with humans, the process should begin as early as possible and certainly no later than two months of age. The key period for learning is up to four months; you haven't got very much time. Left any later and the cat will probably never feel completely at ease among owners and their friends. This is also why it is virtually impossible to tame a foundling wild cat older than six or seven months. Under that age it is no more difficult than with domestic cats – I've done it with lions and pumas – but the troubles arise when the big cat eventually has to return to its fellows in the zoo or wild life park. Reintegration then needs much patience and expert handling, but, on the other hand, what else can you do? You can't keep a grown lion living in the house. What would the neighbours say?

Feline foster mothers

If you are looking for a foster mother, make enquiries at the local animal shelter, veterinary surgeons office and breeders. There are also orphan kitten rescue organizations dotted around the world which can offer expert help and advice. A foster mother does not need to be the same breed as the orphans and if, as is normally the case, she has kittens of her own, they should on no account be more than two weeks older than the orphan. Otherwise there is a considerable risk that the newcomer at the milk bar will get pushed out and knocked about.

Fostering across species

Domestic queens will sometimes foster the young of other species. I well remember a cross-bred tabby at Windsor Safari Park bringing up a pair of cheetah cubs whose mother had died suddenly from a massive abdominal haemorrhage whilst giving birth to them. She had nowhere near enough milk for them (they were given milk substitute from a bottle) but provided them with those other maternal essentials: attention, licking and warmth for a vital few weeks. A year later I was utterly delighted to watch the two cheetahs, now almost fully grown and towering above her, following dutifully behind their 'Mum' as she walked proudly and unconcernedly across their reserve, tail held high as ever, instructing them to 'follow me'. The cheetah keepers allowed her in each day for about an hour, so that she could check up on her 'foster kids' and spend some time lying snuggled up in the grass with them. There are also several instances where cats have been employed to raise leopard cats (logical in view of the antecedents of the Bengal breed), ferrets, rabbits and, once, hedgehogs. (I should explain that baby hedgehogs start out with pliable, soft spines.)

Human foster mothers

When, despite all your efforts at finding one, a feline foster mother is not available, then a human must do the fostering instead. This necessitates giving the kittens all the attention that their mother would have, trying as best as you can to mimic all the things a queen does for her brood, including stroking and gently massaging the body muscles and limbs and cleaning ears, mouths and bums.

Toilet stimulating regime

Using wet wipes or some pieces of cotton wool that have been dampened in warm water, the kittens' genital and anal areas should be rubbed in order to stimulate bladder and bowel movement. Do this, as their mother would, before and, again, around fifteen minutes after feeding, but note that bowel movements may take a day or two to get started in the new-born. The kitten may give a little distress cry before voiding – don't worry, this is quite normal. You will need to continue your 'toilet stimulating regime' for about four weeks.

Staying warm

Kittens that are deprived now of their mother's warm fur, should at all times be kept snug. A heat lamp or electric heating pad, which must be wrapped in some flannel or a towel, is an essential piece of nursing equipment. The air temperature in the box or cat bed where the kittens spend their time, should be kept at between 31–33°C (89–93°F) night and day for newborns, reducing to between 27°C (81°F) and 29°C (84°F) at two weeks of age and to between 23°C (75°F) and 27°C (81°F) from three weeks onwards.

Using a litter tray

The kittens should be trained eventually to receive their food on cue and to use their litter tray. From about three weeks of age, the urinating and defaecating reflexes will be triggered when the kittens go onto the litter. A small quantity of soiled litter should always be left when you are cleaning the tray, as the smell of it will remind the kittens what they are there for. Never physically punish a kitten (or a cat of any age for that matter) if it fails to use the tray. Absolutely no rubbing noses in droppings or any of that nonsense.

Dominant kittens

Bullying among kittens, orphan or not, can begin in the first few days of life. Dominant tendencies start to assert themselves surprisingly early. Muffin and Mitzi, two of my Birmans that were bred in my house, are a good example of this. By two days of age, Muffin, the male, was energetically elbowing his sister Mitzi out of the way at suckling time. Now six years old, he shows no sign of bullying whatsoever. It's just that food was, is, and probably always will be, his main interest in life. He is a genetically programmed gourmand, and, no, he is not (yet) obese.

Single, hand-reared kittens, while developing good social relationships with human beings, may lack any knowledge of how to respond to and handle other members of their own species. In a multi-cat household, this may lead to them not tolerating other cats gladly. Quite a number of orphan cats raised without sibling contact, or not being given consistent human attention, develop a nervous disposition and, in my view, it is best for them not to be in a home with other cats.

Summary

As you can see from all this, the Thinking Cat would appear to have a social conscience (can I use the word 'humanitarian'?) and absolutely no trace of racism! OK, I'll admit it is, in fact, instinctive. The fact remains that domestic queens make exceedingly good mothers.

We have talked about orphan kittens, but what about feline mothers who lose their offspring for one reason or another? They do often show signs of grieving – restlessly searching for the missing kittens, vocalizing, calling for them to come, sometimes going off their food and, in general, appearing distinctly preoccupied.

Normally this behaviour passes off after a few days but, in rare cases, medication by the veterinarian, prescribing tranquillizers, is called for. However, it is not necessary, nor free of potential side effects, to give drugs to 'get rid of the milk'; with no kittens suckling, the milk production will wind down automatically.

Coping with feline foibles and faults

Yes the Rum Tum Tugger is a Curious Cat –
And there isn't any need for me to spout it:
For he will do
As he do do
And there's no doing anything about it!
T. S. Eliot, Old Possum's Book of Practical Cats

The majority of cat owners will experience some form of problem with their pet's behaviour during their lifetime. It may be a minor oddity or something much more worrying. The causes of these upsets or phenomena are many and varied. Whereas some are the fault of the owners, others are psychological ones arising either in the mind of an individual animal or in wider cat society. Natural feline physiology or ancient instinct lie at the root of some and there are also those that are medical conditions in disguise. I will outline many of these problems and suggest what the owner might do to at least alleviate or, with luck, totally eradicate them.

Changes in character of the cat

Let us look first at general changes that might take place in the character or temperament of the cat for no obvious reason. This can happen in animals of any age but are rather commoner in the old. Of course, a cat that was once even-tempered and relaxed but is now anxious, jittery, even plainly scared to death of something it alone can perceive, may have had an unpleasant experience of which you are unaware. An attack by a dog or an act of ill treatment by a human being while out of the house, a firework landing in the garden when you are away for the evening or a lamp bulb exploding close to it might be the cause. The effects on the animal of such things, though sometimes quite dramatic, are generally short-lived and, if sufficient to cause the owner concern, can be easily alleviated by the veterinarian prescribing such medication as Valium.

The ageing cat

Gradual, more permanent alterations in temperament can affect cats as they grow old. The slow process of ageing of nerve cells and nerve fibres in the brain is behind it. These changes are not usually troubling

105

to the owner. Like people, the cats are less active, more steady and, often, more tolerant with the advancing years. But some individuals become more nervous and withdrawn just because they realise their powers are fading; their ability to cope with affairs, particularly in feline social relationships, is weakening. Such cats must be given extra dollops of loving attention and kept involved, without pushing and harassing them, in the life of the family.

We all know the old person who, since retirement, has become rather bitter, grouchy and grumpy. The same can happen to an old cat. It may grumble, even spit or lash out tetchily with a paw if disturbed, particularly while sleeping. Again, such characters should be handled with understanding and tact. Tender loving care should always be on the menu.

Most of these sudden or gradual changes in behaviour can be greatly ameliorated by nothing more than paying thoughtful attention to the animal. Talking to a cat is not a sentimental nonsense. Repeated words become recognized. A range of tones – gentle, friendly,

Mousing memories

While old cats can no longer engage in the hunting adventures of their youth, at least not with much chance of success, many still seem to dream of the old mousing or birding days. (An exception was Mickey, a Lancashire factory cat who was killing mice right up until his death in 1968 at twenty-three years of age. His lifetime total of 'kills' was over 22,000). From time to time, they cannot resist the inclinations of yesteryear and an owner's ball of wool or a grape dropped onto the carpet will elicit a spark of the old stalk and pounce.

It should be encouraged to keep fit in this and other ways just as retired folk are recommended to take some suitable physical exercise like walking or Tai Chi. Equip the venerable cat with some of the things it used to enjoy as a kitten and which can now, once again, give him pleasure and stimulate easy movement – soft toys, ping pong balls and, especially, boxes. Cats adore boxes.

sympathetic, congratulatory and encouraging – are similarly taken on board. The Thinking Cat is intelligent. His name epitomizes his individuality. His name means something to him.

In the same way, handling, stroking, carrying and gentle patting count to a cat. Of course, your initial approach should be cautious to a degree, respecting your cat's feelings and without any 'pushiness' on your part. There should never be any demonstration of exasperation on your part if the cat indicates that he is not quite ready for intimacy by pulling away and retreating into a corner. Patience and persistence are called for.

Giving little treats is always a good ploy. Above all, you must be consistent and regular in your attention, not all fuss one day and oblivious to the cat the next. Consistency, routine, regularity in all things – these are what appeal to the feline nature. Erratic fluctuations in your attitude to the pet are disconcerting and may, by creating uncertainty and anxiety in the cat's mind, be highly counter-productive.

The more staid and respectable the character of the elderly Puss, the more it is likely to be accompanied by the conservative outlook on life and forgetfulness that I mentioned earlier. Rearrangement of the furniture in the house is frowned upon: there may be occasional toilet 'accidents', and a reluctance or inability to work the cat flap. This latter is often, I suspect, at least with my Birmans, a wicked delight in getting the owner trained to open the door to outside instead. Idleness, in other words, but as ever we excuse it.

Any tendency for old timers to wander off has to be treated seriously. They may well have to be loosely supervised whenever out of doors, should always wear a collar and disc bearing their name and address, and must be indoors at night.

Many pensioner cats discover to their satisfaction, and thereafter, play on, the fact that owners respond more indulgently to their 'new' quieter, more tranquil and less demanding personality. They assume the role of benign feline sage in place of dashing cat-about-town. Owners seem to like it, and the cats get more spoiled – an excellent arrangement.

Physical factors

It is most important that owners do not assume that any changes in demeanour or temperament are always necessarily due to some 'natural' cause such as age or sex. Physical disease may be the reason for a cat becoming uncharacteristically dull and withdrawn or unduly exited. A pet that is suddenly jumpy, nervy and over-excitable might have been poisoned by, for example, slug bait pellets, organochlorine insecticide or a snakebite. One that is displaying acute sensitivity to being touched, almost to the point of going into spasms, might have eaten strychnine-laced bait, rodent poison or, more easily, a poisoned rodent. On the other hand, it could be that it is an early sign of the animal having contracted tetanus (lockjaw), peritonitis or an acute under-skin septic infection following a bite from another cat, perhaps some days previously. If in any doubt as to what these phenomena might represent, consult your vet without delay.

Apparent alterations in feline temperament may be associated with disease of, age-related degeneration in, or accidental damage to, the sense organs. The two principal ones, naturally, are deafness and blindness.

Deafness

In cats, this can be congenital, as in white cats with blue eyes, a result of the gradual degenerative changes that take place in the ageing feline ear or due to disease of various kinds. Signs of deafness are a lack of response to well-known words, its name being called and so forth, or, more worryingly, to the sounds of approaching danger, such as a barking dog, lawnmower or motor vehicle.

The congenital and senile types of deafness are not amenable to treatment. All deaf cats should be kept either completely indoors or with access only to an enclosed garden or yard. It is easy to continue to communicate with a deaf cat using sign language. Simple hand signals can indicate 'Come here', 'No' and 'Jump up here', for example. Deaf cats learn just as quickly as hearing cats under training by sound or voice cues, and they will catch on to the system simply through repetition of the signals during daily life without any formal training sessions. My sister-in-law, Niki, has made effortless and rapid progress in interacting with her old, stone-deaf tabby, Cagney, in this way.

Diseases of the ear

The diseases of the ear that can cause deafness are various. They include excessive build-up of waxy secretions in the ear canal – easy to clean out with swabs or twists of cotton wool dipped in warmed olive oil; heavy infestations of the cat ear mite parasite, *Otodectes*, tiny 'insects' that can be eradicated by the use of ear mange drops obtainable from your vet or

Sexually related changes

Apparent changes in temperament, but which are transient, also frequently occur in relation to a cat's sexual activity. Queens become restless, more vocal and plaintive during oestrus, but also tend to indulge in bouts of increased real, or possibly mock, affection towards the owner. Toms are equally restless and anxious to be out and about if there is a queen on heat in the vicinity. During late pregnancy and more especially after giving birth, a queen will usually become increasingly aggressive towards males, whether other members of the household or outsiders. Nursing queens may even attack, at the drop of a hat, another cat of either sex, or a dog.

pet shop; and infections which, particularly when chronic, often lead to thickening of the ear canal walls and accumulation of inflammatory fluid or pus, so obstructing hearing.

Ear infections, severe mite infestations or mixtures of both need veterinary attention, and this may involve examination by use of an auriscope, laboratory culture of an ear swab sample, and treatment with antibiotics and/or antifungal medications. A few advanced chronic cases may require surgery. Regular weekly inspection and, if necessary, cleaning of the cat's ears with cotton wool and a little olive oil, should be carried out by owners throughout the animal's life to prevent such problems arising.

Blindness

This can come on suddenly, causing the cat to bump into objects repeatedly before becoming rather bemused and withdrawn. Gradual blindness may not present many obvious signs to the owner unless there are visible alterations to be seen in the cat's eyes like greatly distended pupils or white or blue colour changes within the eyes. Slow loss of sight gives the animal time to adjust and rely even more on its other senses and may, in any case, never progress to total absence of vision.

Provided the cat doesn't have to move house and there is no major rearrangement of furniture or altered location of litter trays and food and water bowls, many cats seem to cope with total blindness, though not as well as dogs, and younger cats are frequently more troubled by the disability than old ones, sometimes becoming distinctly apathetic or nervous. Blindness in just one eye is of little consequence to any cat.

Conditions causing blindness

Eye conditions that can cause blindness include severe chronic inflammation of the cornea (chronic keratitis), opacity of the lens (cataract), retinal disease or detachment, tumours of the eye or optical areas of the brain, and serious eye injuries. Some of these are treatable by veterinary science. There are appropriate medical or surgical procedures for the range of corneal diseases, and cataractous lenses can be removed surgically. Where dense cataracts affect both eyes, it is usually only necessary to operate on one. The cat will have enough vision restored to resume a normal life with no need for spectacles or contact lenses in its case. Where this type of eye surgery is indicated it is best performed by one of the specialist veterinary ophthalmologists of whom there are now quite a number dotted around Britain.

Any sign of undue redness of the membranes around the eye or under the eyelids (conjunctivae), purulent or excessive watery discharge, soreness and partial closure of the eyelids, or pale bluish or whitish haziness of the clear part of the eye (cornea) in a cat of any age should be given prompt veterinary attention to avoid the possible development of sight-threatening complications.

Behavioural spin-offs

There are a number of conditions that, while not behavioural in themselves, are associated with or, in some cases, caused by, a cat's behaviour. These conditions include furballs, overgrown dewclaws, bad breath, and drinking and waterworks problems.

Furballs

Furballs, accretions of hair, in the form of dense masses that often resemble cocktail sausages in size and shape, build up gradually in the stomachs of many cats, particularly longhaired and semi-longhaired breeds, though shorthairs are not immune to their formation. They are most common in cats that groom themselves or other cats excessively for whatever reason, be it psychological in cases of obsessive-compulsive behaviour, or physical as when itchy skin disease is present.

The furballs are normally vomited up after a few preliminary, often noisy, retches, a process that, in most cases, leaves the animal none the worse for wear. Some cats, like my neutered queen, Golda, bring up the balls regularly, as often perhaps as once a week and despite, as in her case, being regularly groomed. Often the furballs are mixed with a small quantity of undigested grass. It is impossible to say whether the cat sometimes does the eating of grass knowingly in order to act as an emetic when it feels its stomach to be bloated by these furry foreign bodies, a sort of self-medication. I suspect it is, although, as we have seen, cats do eat grass and other vegetables for other reasons.

Symptoms

An owner can often predict when a furball-regurgitating episode is imminent. The cat's appetite understandably diminishes as available space in the stomach is steadily reduced. There may also be constipation and visible distension of the abdomen. If the ball or balls remain for long in the stomach there can be noticeable loss of weight.

Treatment

After the furball has been expelled, appetite usually returns quickly to normal. In some cases, however, where inappetance is pronounced and lasts for several days, veterinary attention is called for. The vet, during his examination, will be able to feel the furball while palpating the abdomen gently with his fingers. X-rays are sometimes used to confirm the nature of the problem. Normally treatment with mineral oil (liquid paraffin) is all that is required, but, in rare cases, a gastrotomy – an operation to open the stomach – has to be performed.

Prevention

As ever, prevention is the watchword. No matter what the underlying cause of the cat ingesting substantial quantities of hair, regular (daily), thorough grooming by the owner, using the special brushes, combs or grooming mittens available from pet shops, is essential. Some proprietary pelleted cat foods are now on the market that are claimed to be helpful in encouraging fur to pass naturally through the digestive tract without concentrating in the stomach. The other animal, in which I have had major problems with furballs, with some growing to the size of an ogen melon, is the camel. The trouble is that camels cannot vomit the things up.

Overgrown dewclaws

Cats that are old, live permanently indoors or, for other reasons, are not very active, tend to develop overgrown claws. The dewclaw on the inside of the 'wrist' is particularly prone to overgrow, as it does not contact the ground. They can frequently be heard tapping along as the cat walks on hard tile or wooden surfaces.

It is often said that when a cat scratches something solid – a tree trunk, fence post, valuable piece of furniture or, best of all, its very own scratching post – that it is 'sharpening its nails'. That is not strictly true. As we have seen, scratching plays an important role in marking territory, ownership and, indeed, its own existence by leaving both visible marks and scent information. Nevertheless, a secondary purpose of scratching is not so much to produce a sharp point to the claw like whetting a fish hook on stone, as to clear away the old, outer husks of the claws which are beginning naturally to split. The well-turned-out Thinking Cat, in other words, is giving itself a manicure.

The claws, of course, are what cause much of the damage when fighting or, unfortunately, when playing amiably with the owner. I wonder how many million pairs of ladies' tights are ruined each year by fun-loving cats and their claws. Every stocking manufacturer must surely have a cat as its mascot.

Clipping a cat's claws

There is an operation, which is not uncommon in the United States, to surgically remove the claws from a cat under anaesthetic. Thankfully, such mutilation is illegal in Great Britain and Australia and is frowned upon in New Zealand. However, clipping a cat's claws is a different matter – humane, painless and easy if done correctly.

Use either very short scissors, human toenail clippers or, best of all, veterinary 'guillotine-type' claw clippers. Hold the animal firmly in your lap and press the pad of its paw to make the claws extend. Examine the claw carefully. Inside the thickest main part is the pinkish-coloured 'quick' that contains both nerves and blood vessels. You must *not* cut this. The white tips are dead tissue and can be cut, but not closer than 2 mm (one-tenth of an inch) to the quick. If in any doubt as to how to trim the claws, ask the vet to show you how, or let him clip them himself.

Lions and tigers in zoos also sometimes have to have their overgrown claws clipped. General anaesthetic delivered by flying dart and extra large clippers are needed in their case.

Bad breath

A prime example of owner and cat unwittingly cooperating in behaviour that causes problems is the very common condition of bad breath or halitosis. By bad breath I am not referring to the warm, fishy smell that you get when Puss jumps up for a nuzzle after polishing off another tin of pilchards. My wife and I rather like that. No, by bad, I mean bad, the odour of the sulphurous gases given off when bacteria are at work on tissue.

What causes it?

Most often seen in old cats, the cause is dental and gum disease that, in turn, is induced by dietary factors for which both cat and owner are responsible. The whole process takes a long time, perhaps years, to arrive at the point where an unpleasant aroma is first noticed when the cat is near by. Slowly a hard yellow-brown deposit (calculus) accumulates on the teeth. Eventually it presses into the margins of the gums and inflammation (gingivitis) follows. Bacteria gain entrance between gum and tooth, gums recede and the tooth socket becomes diseased. Besides the smell, the cat will exhibit signs of tenderness or pain in the mouth, will resent having its mouth opened and have difficulty in eating. Teeth may eventually drop out. Long-term mouth pathology of this sort can lead in some cases to disease developing elsewhere in the body, such as the kidneys.

Preventing calculus formation

Some pet cats, of course, do dine every now and then on whole, raw prey, but the majority subsist on pet food. Preferred, naturally, by the owner and selected carefully by the cat which so often shows an inclination to become progressively fussier as it grows older, the proprietary food, although it is nutritionally balanced, vitaminized, enticingly flavoured and offered in jelly, pâté, gravy, semi-moist or pelleted forms, does not clean the teeth.

Wild cats

While common in domestic cats, dental troubles are rare in wild cats. Why? It's all to do with feeding. Folk often say that 'eating bones keeps an animal's teeth clean'. Not so – cracking bones won't stop calculus build-up. What does keep tigers' and other wild felines' teeth and gums healthy is the eating of raw flesh, including skin, gristle and muscle, as well as bone. When the teeth pierce skin and muscle these tissues automatically slide along the tooth enamel and physically clean it. Splintering bone cannot do that.

The only wild animal patients of mine that get daily brushing (with aloes toothpaste) to prevent calculus are the fine breeding group of killer whales at Marineland Antibes in France. As with most domestic cats, their teeth don't get cleaned and polished by killing things; they simply swallow the tens of kilos of prime herring and mackerel poured into their mouths several times a day!

Quite the opposite is true, in fact, as tinned food is particularly likely to leave a film of sticky foodstuff on the cat's teeth which, in time, will become calcified, hard and difficult to remove.

Feline tooth and gum troubles will always be with us and we are unlikely to improve matters by giving our pets a daily fresh-killed rat or pigeon. Cooked tripe and 'lights' (sheep or pig lungs) used to be very good at keeping cats' teeth in good order, but nowadays, alas, few owners want to cook such offal, many cats would turn up their noses at it, and, anyway, since the arrival of BSE tripe is not so easy to come by.

Regular dental inspections

The prevention of calculus formation should be every owner's aim throughout the lifetime of their pet, and thus the cat should have its mouth inspected regularly and the teeth brushed at least once a week with either salt and some warm water or one of the special veterinary tooth pastes that are now available, using the cat's own soft-bristled tooth brush. Some pelleted foods are now formulated so as to assist in polishing the teeth while they are being chewed.

Dental treatment

Dental disease in the cat will need veterinary treatment which, in the case of simple calculus, means cracking off the built-up material by means of surgical tooth-scaling instruments or an ultra-sonic machine under sedation. More advanced and complicated mouth conditions can involve different types of dentistry, extractions and the administration of anti-bacterial drugs.

Drinking problems and cats

No, I am not suggesting that the Thinking Cat would ever hit the bottle. Dogs and parrots that are partial to beer are not unknown, and in my hometown of Rochdale I once had to deal with a pet monkey addicted to the Advocaat brand of egg flip. But cats in Alcoholics Anonymous meetings? Emphatically no! What I am referring to is the complaint by cat owners from time to time that their pet is either drinking too much or, apparently, too little.

Drinking too much

An increase in thirst in the cat can be a sign of diabetes, of either the sugar diabetes or the water diabetes form (diabetes insipidus). The former type, which is caused by the malfunction of cells in the pancreas, is commoner by far than the latter, which is of pituitary gland origin. Sugar diabetes is often also associated with an increase in appetite which is accompanied, paradoxically, by loss of weight, increased output of urine, depression and, sometimes, rapidly developing cataracts in the lenses of the eyes. Laboratory tests will show excessive levels of sugar in the cat's blood and urine.

Treatment of sugar diabetes is usually very effective and can involve adjustment of the affected cat's diet (high protein and absolutely minimum carbohydrate), the injection of insulin daily (simple and painless to do when shown how by the vet) or, in some suitable cases, the administration of anti-diabetic tablets by mouth.

Diabetes insipidus also causes increased drinking and urination. I have never seen a case in a cat, domestic or wild. My last two insipidus patients were Chu-Lin, King Juan Carlos of Spain's giant panda, and a camel in a wildlife park, also in Spain. Like cats with the disease, both of these were treated successfully with diuretic drugs that actually are designed to increase urine output, a surprising, paradoxical therapy but one also employed in humans with the same condition.

Drinking too little

What do we mean by drinking too little? Provided fresh clean water or milk (the latter is not essential) is available at all times, the cat is not likely to become dehydrated. Water is necessary for life and all animals obtain their water from three sources – by drinking, by eating water-containing food and by making it themselves within their bodies while metabolizing (processing) food they have eaten. For bigger creatures, like humans and horses, drinking is the most important source of water. Smaller animals obtain important additional amounts of water from food, particularly the flesh of their prey if they are carnivores or piscivores (fish-eaters). The smallest animals get all the water they require by burning carbohydrates, fats and, if necessary, protein during the normal digestion and processing of their food. House mice can survive happily without drinking. We produce so-called metabolic water in the same way, but in proportion to our size and requirements, it is nowhere near enough.

We saw earlier that cats can concentrate their urine, and so lose less of it in getting rid of waste products, than human beings. The wild sand cats, which apparently do not need to drink, conserve water by restricting their activities to nighttime, avoiding the heat of the day by resting in the burrows they excavate. Some domestic cats, particularly those on tinned cat food, get enough water from that combined with their metabolic water not to necessitate drinking very much, if at all. (Take a look at the analysis on the label of your cat's favourite food. The water content is generally around 80 per cent; four-fifths of the tin or packet you buy is water. Not cheap!)

Cats on mainly dry foods and toms that were castrated early, when the size of the penis and water pipe (urethra) within it were quite small, can have trouble when their concentrated urine precipitates minerals in the form of salt crystal 'gravel' in the bladder. This can block the urethra and cause painful obstruction to the urine flow that can only be alleviated by veterinary treatment that may involve catheterization or even an operation.

Prevention

This is twofold – always to provide fresh water for the cat, with the addition of a light sprinkling of table salt for cats with a history of blockage in order to stimulate liquid intake, and to delay castration of toms until they are at least six months of age, thereby allowing the urethra more time to grow in diameter.

Waterworks and similar problems

One of the commonest behavioural problems seen in cats and of which owners vociferously complain is the 'toilet accident' in the house – urinating or defecating in some totally improper spot. It's as if the animal suddenly loses all its litter tray training. Why do such incidents occur?

The first thing to eliminate as a possible cause of indoor urination or stool-passing is the existence of some kind of medical problem. Kidney disease or the two types of diabetes can increase the output of urine dramatically and bladder inflammation (cystitis) due to infection or the irritation of the membrane lining the bladder by crunchy gravel often makes the act of urination painful for the cat. As a consequence, the animal passes water irregularly, whenever it can, and frequently in the wrong place.

A normal cat associates urination with its litter tray. So, when urination becomes painful it may 'blame' the tray and decline to use it. 'I'll try peeing in a place that perhaps won't make it hurt' I imagine the cat thinks.

Defecation out of the tray may likewise be due to some form of bowel upset, particularly diarrhoea. The animal may not have time to get to the tray before the 'accident' happens. Owners should check the appearance of the stools. Diarrhoea, which can come in a range of colours, may be

Pensioner cats

Elderly cats, but by no means the majority, may develop 'accidental' tendencies when very old. As sometimes happens with elderly people, the contracting sphincter muscles of the urinary tract and anus can become unreliable and, on occasion, rather too relaxed. Weakening hormonal control of bladder activity can also play a part. Not much can be done about this geriatric class of accident except to forgive an old friend and companion, forget – and clean up. Because cats are inherently most fastidious and clean in their habits and house-training is deeply ingrained in old ones, the vast majority of 'accidental' incidents in elderly cats are caused by physical/medical changes in their bodies. The aforementioned senile forgetfulness is the opposite of thinking. Old cats never begin actively to think 'dirty'.

caused by infections, parasites, food or digestive factors. If it lasts more than, at the most, forty-eight hours, seek veterinary advice.

If a cat is seen apparently straining when crouching to urinate with no or only fitful drops of urine being expressed, a visit to the vet is called for. Left untreated, bladder disease can become chronic and extremely difficult to eradicate, and it can lead to serious, even fatal, complications. Any case of sudden unexplained 'toilet accidents' coming out of the blue warrants a medical check-up before assuming it must be a psychological disturbance.

Litter-tray training breakdowns

Psychological causes of litter-tray training breaking down are many and varied. Some are due to the actions of the owner, some to cat-to-cat social relationships, some to sex rearing its ugly head and some to the existence of indefinable sources of stress. The sort of questions owners should ask themselves in this situation are these:

■ Is the litter tray 'putting the cat off' in some way? Has the litter material been changed to one that is not to Puss's liking? Some cats detest the chlorophyll odour-eating compounds added to some types of litter.

■ Has someone in the house recently scolded or alarmed the cat when it was on its tray? Such an incident could have a negative reinforcement effect on a normally well-toilet-trained animal.

■ Is the litter being changed and the tray cleaned out often enough?

■ Has a strong-smelling disinfectant been used in cleaning the tray? Scrubbing with soap or washing-up liquid and water is sufficient.

■ In a multi-cat household, is one more submissive individual being threatened or harassed by another while on the tray? Is another cat perhaps denying it access to the tray, especially by blocking the doorway of the covered type of tray?

■ Has the litter tray been moved to a place that is less congenial to peaceful, reflective voiding? Putting it near food dishes, in an area where children play, or where the dog likes to hang out, or where there is too much noise and movement in general, can deter the toilet user.

■ Are there enough litter trays for each cat in a multi-cat household to have one for its own use? It is best, in addition, to have one extra tray. Cats abhor queuing for the bathroom. Of course, if cats have access to outdoors, a multiplicity of litter trays will not be necessary. My five moggies are clean as whistles with just one litter tray in my office, which they seldom use, and then only to urinate, and a cat flap, open day and night, that lets them out to the back garden.

■ Is the cat getting too plump and portly to pass with ease through the doorway of a covered tray?

■ Is an old cat, one perhaps troubled with rheumatism or aching joints, finding it more difficult now to go upstairs to a litter tray on another floor or even, in some cases, just to step over the sides of a tray if they are too high?

■ Did the cat inadvertently get shut in or was it, in some way, denied access to its litter tray?

Stress and anxiety are major causes of toilet-training misdemeanours. Moving house, the rearrangement of furniture, having workmen in, the arrival of new household members, whether a baby, a dog or another cat – these are the sort of things that may stress a cat.

Spraying urine

This must be distinguished from simple urination at a place other than in the litter tray; it is something the cat elects to do rather than being compelled to do by mounting bladder pressure and is not just confined to entire toms. It is also seen in neutered toms and, less commonly, in females, and is essentially a marking of territory or property-ownership, a piece of olfactory advice to other cats. The animal backs up to a usually vertical surface, raises its tail, causes its rear end to quiver, makes treading movements with its back feet, and ejects a small quantity of urine backwards. This performance is commoner in multi-cat households where competition, particularly between males, often exists. It is a sign of anxiety in a cat that feels its personal living-space, its own familiar objects, to be under threat from a usurper. Typically this can be where an outside cat enters the house through a cat flap, usually in search of food. The resident cat, alarmed at the invasion, feels that it must indicate in the strongest possible (strongest smelling!) terms to whom this place, these contents belong. Sex in the vicinity, a queen coming into oestrus or an entire tom leaving an odorous visiting card on the doorstep can cause similar 'accidental' reactions.

Solving the problem

What can be done about all this? The owner should ask the questions outlined above, and, if any ring bells, take appropriate steps to put things right. We will consider how to handle cats when there are new arrivals in the home later. Neutering all toms or queens in the household will often help where sex is a factor, but neutered animals frequently spray, too. One other great effect of neutering toms is that their urine loses its characteristic pungent smell. Places where a cat urinates or defecates should be thoroughly cleaned with a proprietary deodorizing liquid and then, hopefully, rendered undesirable from the cat's point of view. Deterrent sprays or mothballs can be put down at the spot.

Some behaviourists recommend that, where feasible, spraying areas might be converted into feeding or playing zones, thus deterring the cat from soiling them. The litter tray could be put in the spraying area and then gradually, by an inch or two a day, moved to where it should be. An alternative is to put the cat's sleeping bed there.

Where the basic problem is more difficult to discern, as with competition and rivalries in the household hierarchy, subliminal conflicts and jealousies, it may be necessary to consider medication using anxiety-alleviating drugs prescribed by the vet. Tranquillizers, like Valium, and drugs more usually given as contraceptives such as medroxyprogesterone (Depo-Provera) and megestrol acetate (Ovarid) have been used successfully to stop spraying in some cases. Unless absolutely essential, I prefer not to use internal drugs of any kind in treating behavioural problems.

Recently, a new and very promising kind of aid in tackling this type of aberrant behaviour has become available in the form of cat pheromone-containing sprays and vaporizers. I have used them with some success both with my Birmans and on a clowder of five shorthairs belonging to a friend in Mallorca. Barely detectable by the human nose and not at all unpleasant, these preparations infuse cat skin gland pheromones into the air where they are picked up by the delicate lining of the feline nostril and pass, via the blood stream, to the brain. The effect, in the majority of, but not all, cats is to stop urine marking and make the animals in general more calm and settled.

Where outsider cats and cat flaps are the problem, it is best to install the type of flap that will only open when your cat, carrying a small and specific magnetic device on its collar, is in close proximity to it.

Footnote

Before leaving the subject of spraying, I must mention two other manifestations of the behaviour. Occasionally a cat will spray on the legs of some member of the family. This what I call the 'I Love You' sort of spraying. By no means associated with stress or anxiety, it is nevertheless quasi-territorial in nature. The cat is marking the human being, affectionately, as being its property, 'mine, all mine' you might say. You either have to put up with this odoriferous token of its feelings or, using the techniques outlined earlier, train it not to be so demonstrative in that particular fashion.

The other kind of spraying, which I entitle the 'Sense of Humour' variety, I have seen only in lions. A classic example was the old male lion at Manchester Zoo who was popular with visitors. He paraded amiably close to the weld-mesh fence where his fans could admire his superb mane and big, dark eyes. From time to time, when a sizeable bunch of folk had gathered to look at him, he would slowly turn so that his rump was facing them. Lions, like other cats, including domestic ones, tigers, leopards and jaguars – but not pumas which squat – urinate backwards and, suddenly, without warning, he would eject a strong stream of urine with great accuracy through the mesh and onto the face or body of someone in the front row. As the Head Keeper, once remarked, 'That lion has got eyes in his arse, I warrant!' How the big cat's audience roared with laughter! The victim, reeking of entire lion urine, which is considerably more potent than that of any thuggish feral tom, would stagger back out of the crowd and another of the still-guffawing onlookers would take up the vacated space. Oh, what a card that lion is, the people said. He was indeed, but little did they know he had another 'card' up his sleeve, or, to be more precise, another round of noisome pee already loaded in the barrel of his penis. Before the laughter had died away he would jet this second helping of urine with perfect reverse aim at his next victim. It wasn't territory marking or anxiety or stress; but rather pure, unadulterated, wicked mischief. Life, for that very definitely Thinking Lion, had its funny moments.

Odd sexual behaviours of cats

We have seen how cats of both sexes can become restless, highly vocal and distracted when sex is in the air. These phenomena are to be regarded as normal, but there are also forms of behaviour related to the animals' sexual make-up that are not.

Hypersexuality

Becoming over-sexed can occur occasionally in both male and female entires. In the male, it manifests itself as incessant questing for sex and is caused by excessive production of the male sex hormone, testosterone, in the testes or malfunction of the brain's cerebral cortex. Hypersexuality has been recorded in laboratory experiments (unfortunately) where cats have been deprived of the opportunity to enter the kind of sleep that is accompanied by rapid eye movements (commonly called REM sleep), and in which dreaming occurs. Although anti-testosterone drugs have been developed (principally to treat human sex offenders) and contraceptive pills, normally given to females, are employed widely in other animal species to reduce male, and female, sexual aggression, the logical cure for hypersexuality in toms is castration.

Queens with hypersexuality exhibit prolonged, pronounced, ever recurring heat periods. The cause is the persistence, without normal rupture, of follicles on the ovaries beyond the time when an oestrus period should have ended. One or more of these follicles may grow into ovarian cysts which produce abnormally large amounts of the female sex hormones called oestrogens. Again, although follicle-bursting hormones and anti-oestrogen medication can be used, the best answer is ovaro-hysterectomy, the spaying of the queen under general anaesthetic.

False or phantom pregnancy

This is not uncommon in bitches but much less so in queens. Here, under the influence of ovarian hormones, the cat behaves, to a remarkable extent, as if she were pregnant. She will be restless, attempt to make a nest with torn pieces of paper or cloth, engage in 'nursing' such objects as shoes, socks or toys to the best of her abilities. Her abdomen may appear to enlarge and she may actually produce milk.

Treatment of false pregnancy is not always necessary. The phenomenon will tend to fade away naturally, though it can take as long as six or eight weeks to do so. If the queen's mammary glands are very enlarged and painful, warm compresses may give relief, and reducing the amount of daily food should help to stem milk production. Should mammary gland pain persist for more than a day or two, or if the animal becomes dull, or there is a liquid discharge from her vulva, it is wise to seek veterinary attention. A queen that repeatedly has false pregnancies is best spayed.

Sexually aroused neutered toms

Owners can be surprised when their neutered toms become sexually aroused when a queen on heat is in the vicinity. It is not uncommon. Two of my neutered Birman toms did it every time my queen was in oestrus before she too was neutered. These cats, unburdened by testicles, went through all the typical male courtship and mating behaviour with her, including mounting and biting the scruff of her neck. The explanation is that there must be some testosterone coming from somewhere in the body although, with spermatozoa no longer able to be produced, the toms cannot impregnate the queen.

One possibility is that during the operation of castration the surgeon's scalpel cuts slightly too close to a testicle, leaving a few hormone-producing cells behind. Another source of testosterone is the adrenal gland for it, in addition to the testes, produces tiny quantities, of male sex hormones in male mammals. I think this latter is the best explanation in most of these cases. Cutting close to the testicle is much more likely to occur in such animals as the horse, and far less likely in the cat. I suppose one or both of these hypotheses of the origin of residual sexual libido may explain the well-recorded fact that the eunuchs who guarded oriental harems in bygone days and, because of their missing organs, were trusted by their masters to behave themselves among the ladies of the court, did in fact often live lives of rather gay abandon.

Gay cats

Talking of gay things and anxious to assure you, dear reader, that although included in this section, I do not consider gay people odd or abnormal in any way, gay cats are certainly unusual and interesting. Homosexual behaviour between two male domestic cats has been reported but, when taken to the extent of going through mating behaviour, is very rare. Some degree of homosexuality has also been recorded by scientists working with Asiatic lions in the famous Gir National Park in India and also with African lions in the Serengeti. There is as yet no consensus of opinion among biologists on what has sometimes been considered to be a temporary behavioural phenomenon. Certainly homosexuality is seen, often quite commonly, among many other animal species.

Great friendship, even what can be described as infatuation of one male domestic cat for another, where usually one of the individuals, frequently to the obvious exasperation of the other, cannot bear to be out of touch with the object of his devoted admiration, is fairly common but cannot be termed homosexual. No mating-type behaviour ever occurs and from time to time the much admired one will swing a paw tetchily or even spit, to indicate that the 'crush' is getting on his nerves. Still, the admirer's attentions continue without wavering, often for a lifetime. Sam, one of my Birmans, has this sort of fixation on another of my males, Sidney.

Queens under siege

Sometimes a neutered queen will continue to be harassed by local entire tomcats. This can result in her becoming nervous and reluctant to go outside. There isn't, unfortunately, much that an owner can do about this except perhaps make the garden or yard safety proof against incoming cats by erecting trellis work or a band of plastic netting along the top of surrounding walls or fences. Attempting to identify the owner, if there is one, of the offending tom or toms and persuading them to have their animals neutered is not easy.

Hermaphrodism

Even rarer than homosexuality is hermaphrodism in the domestic cat. Hermaphrodite cats can possess both a testis and an ovary, a penis and a vagina. As you might expect, the animal's behaviour is that of a mixture of the sexes, with heat periods and all the associated rigmarole of rolling, calling and provocation and then, at other times, the naked aggression of a fighting entire tom.

Cryptorchidism

Occasionally, but less often than in dogs, one or both of a cat's testicles will not descend into the scrotum. This is cryptorchidism. Where that happens the cat will continue to behave like an entire tom, under the influence of the male sex hormone constantly being produced by the wrongly positioned testicles, which may be halfway down a gully leading to the scrotum and called the inguinal canal, or even higher up in the pelvic cavity. Such a cat is not likely to be fertile but it will, in most cases, show all the characteristics, good and bad, of the un-neutered male. If only a single testicle descends correctly, there is little point in having that one removed surgically. Nothing will be achieved while the other organ remains hidden away. A deeper and more complicated operation than normal castration can be performed by the veterinary surgeon on such cryptorchid cats.

Unusual tortoise-shells

A widely held belief, even among cat breeders, is that all tortoise-shell cats must be female, and all gingers are male. It isn't true, for there are occasional interesting exceptions. The sex, colour and pattern of coat, and the physical and mental characteristics of an animal are designated at the outset, in the fertilized egg, by the particular mix of chromosome genetic material received from both parents. Occasionally an unusual chromosome make-up results which is then followed by the birth of a 'curiosity' cat. Less than one in 10,000 tortoise-shell cats are males. Some are fertile; others not. It is possible that there is a disproportionate number of male tortoise- shells among Maine Coons.

Very occasionally, a seemingly male tortoise-shell cat is actually a female. Genetically a total female, it is born with the external physical features of a tom due to something going wrong with hormonal control during the development of the embryo. Some of these 'false males' later go on to act as the females they truly are.

A famous case, with the opposite features, was Skipper, a black-and-orange calico Japanese cat, who, in the 1980s, though bearing normal male genitalia, at one-year-old had the general body shape and face of a female. An extremely quiet and calm fellow, he was uninterested in females in heat, did not spray and did not object when toms, who found him attractive, mounted him. Indeed, when that happened, he would readily adopt the typical female mating posture and chirrup away happily. Although he was not interested in fighting with toms, he frequently battled with females and he was usually the one that instigated the set-to. By the time he was two- and-a-half years old, Skipper had begun to change. Instead of scrapping with other females, he now began to show sexual interest in them and also to spray. His tomcat sex drive was not very strong, however, and his matings with females lacked machismo. He never successfully impregnated any. We do not know what Skipper's detailed sex organ anatomy was or his chromosome make-up. It seems likely that although his external genitalia were male, his brain was genetically female. Maybe he also possessed some quantity at least of ovarian tissue in his abdomen.

Hyposexualism

There are a large number of causes of infertility in cats, including diseases that I shall not deal with here. Hyposexualism is the absence of, or unusually weak, sexual activity in the cat. Rarely, the sex organs are either absent or imperfectly formed. In a multi-cat household, an infertile tom may mate with females and so stimulate ovulation which then results in the following two months of pseudo-pregnancy with no heat periods being exhibited. Another cause is failure of the master gland, the pituitary in the brain, to do its job of organizing oestrus cycles, and there are some medications that can have the side effect of suppressing heats.

In the early 1970s the Manchester zoo where I was consultant vet, sent a pair of lions to Glasgow Zoo. In due course, a cub was born to them, a unique youngster indeed. Ranger, as he was named, was partly black in colour, the first so-called melanistic African lion definitely known to have existed. Sadly the black fur wasn't the only genetic anomaly that Ranger was carrying. He also turned out to be infertile, even though he had a normal sex drive and frequently mated with a female who was known to be fertile, having had a litter of cubs previously.

Interaction with people

Yet another example of the cat's superiority in sophisticated behaviour over that of the dog is in the total lack of quasi-sexual interaction with humans. Where dogs, not infrequently when the mood takes them, will mount the leg of the vicar when he comes to call on a pastoral visit, thrusting away outrageously and threatening to upset the poor cleric's cup of tea, cats would not contemplate such an act of vulgarity. Cats, endowed though they are with a fine sense of smell, would never ram their noses in our

Winged cats

One of the most fascinating tortoise-shells was accidentally shot in Derbyshire in 1897 after being mistaken for a fox. This cat was not only a tortoise-shell tom but also, according to a local newspaper report, 'had fully grown pheasant wings projecting from each side of its fourth rib'! It is certain that the 'wings' were not true feathered appendages, but another extremely rare congenital deformity that causes scaly growths to sprout from the skin.

groin, dog-fashion, in search of some beguiling pheromone. The only exotic animal species that has, with me, engaged in such enthusiastic groin probing, is the giant South American otter. A male at the Zoo de La Casa de Campo in Madrid frightened me considerably each time I had to climb down into his outdoor pen to examine him. He really thrust his nose in hard, and I couldn't but keep worrying about the big, sharp, glistening fangs situated just below that nose. As I said at the time, 'God save my cojones'. If he gave even one small bite... Better not to think about it and get out as quickly as possible! Sure enough, one day a fellow who was not authorized to enter the giant otter installation did so 'to stroke the charming creature'. Thereupon the male otter, after, as was his wont, forcefully investigating the newly arrived groin, went a bit further and ripped out a considerable amount of the man's nether parts. No, give me cats; they have class.

Feline fears, phobias and aggression

> *'Alf Todd,' said Ukridge, soaring to an impressive burst of imagery, 'has about as much chance as a one-armed blind man in a dark room trying to shove a pound of melted butter into a wild cat's left ear with a red-hot needle.'*
> P.G.Wodehouse, Ukridge

Wodehouse, in his inimitable style, is describing a hypothetical incident that would be certain to strike the utmost terror into any Thinking Cat. That being the case, butter-laden red-hot needles in practice seem seldom to

High-level living

A unique and very different sort of sexual oddity among cats, if you can call her that, was Mincha, the black queen who lived in Buenos Aires, Argentina, in the 1950s. She decided, on the spur of the moment one day, that she preferred raising litters of kittens 'on high' rather at pedestrian ground level. So, she thereupon climbed a twelve-metre (forty-foot) high tree and stayed there – for eight years, without ever once descending! During that time, provided with food by well-wishing humans, including a milkman, who raised food and milk up to her by means of ladders and long poles, she gave birth to four litters of healthy kittens. History does not record whether the toms were also elevated to do their duty with the aid of poles, or got there somehow of their own accord. The kittens, it seems, generally returned, once weaned, to terra firma.

generate outbreaks of fear and loathing in the daily lives of our pets, I'm glad to say, but many other things often do. The fears, phobias and aggressive behaviour patterns of cats have each a range of causes and all three of them can, in some circumstances, be linked. Fear is the unpleasant sensation caused by the nearness of danger or pain, whereas a phobia is a lasting dislike or abnormal fear. An ailurophobe is a person who dislikes cats, not necessarily someone who has a fear of them. This distinction in terms similarly applies to cats but there are areas of overlapping.

Objects, other living things, or events may generate a cat's fears. Objects may be such mundane items as vacuum cleaners or cat carrying baskets. Muffin, one of my bunch, is inordinately scared of kitchen foil. The characteristic metallic sound as it is handled sends him scurrying. Fears like this are not rational – Muffin has never been physically hurt by foil – but neither is a person's fear of spiders, which exists even though one has never bitten them, or had one run up their sleeve.

This kind of fear is perhaps more of a phobia. Many cats are frightened of dogs at times but don't have a phobia towards the canine species. A dog at even a reasonably close distance, paying them no attention, does not alarm them. They will watch it but I doubt if their heart rates accelerate very much. If, however, a dog is looking at them, approaching or, in any way, appearing to pose a present threat, they are quick to 'become fearful'. This applies equally with other cats, which may or may not be signalling in one way or another that they are looking for trouble. Aggression and fear are closely linked in the feline life.

Coping with fear

Firstly, how to deal with the fear of things like those travelling baskets? These innocuous containers are not, in themselves, painful or, in most cases, uncomfortable, let alone threatening – except that in the cat's mind there is a threat: of yet another trip to the vet or boarding kennel. The Thinking Cat connects the basket with needle pricks or strange people taking care of him in premises that he doesn't like which are full of sounds, sights and smells that are not those of his accustomed, cosy, very satisfying, normal daily life.

Owners should select travelling containers with care. Some unsettle a cat much less than others, and each cat may have its own preferences. One cat may be happier in the sort of basket where it can look out and see what's going on while another will prefer to be completely in the dark. A spacious well-lined container is always likely to be better received than one of the spartan, cardboard box sort.

Leave the cat container, open, somewhere in the house where the cat can explore and get used to it, maybe even use it as a regular sleeping place. It will become part of the animal's familiar environment and impregnated with its scent. Giving food treats in it will enhance its appeal. This sort of approach will work with other objects that are a source of fear to a cat.

The actual visit to the vet's premises is, of course, often fear-inducing, even if the cat is merely examined gently without any brandishing of instruments of torture, such as thermometers, stethoscopes or, shades of the Inquisition, a hypodermic syringe. It can help to make an appointment at the end of the consulting hours when the waiting room is fairly empty or to wait with the cat in your car until the vet is ready to see it. For really nervous cats who 'get in a state' at such times, a light sedative may be given before leaving home.

Nervous cats

Muffin's phobia for kitchen foil isn't much of a problem for us. He just scarpers for a little while into another room when sea bass en cocotte is being prepared for baking or the Christmas turkey dressed in the stuff. Far more important phobias can affect the very nervous type of cat – to whom the world in general is alarming. Whereas most pets are easy-going, cool customers, this individual takes fright at anything or anybody – anytime. Such cats are agoraphobic, detesting open spaces, and extraordinarily averse to changes in their surroundings. Visitors, new household appliances that make some sort of noise or emit light, sudden bursts of laughter, logs crackling – these and a hundred other things terrify the cat and it darts for a safe, dark hidey-hole, often under a sideboard where it can only just squeeze. Life for these cats is distressing and tends to get more so, sometimes to the point where the animal is hiding most of the day, only coming out to eat during the night. It is equally distressing for an owner to have a pet that agonizes in this way.

Possible causes

The roots of this extreme and unfortunate nervousness are often to be found in the kitten's early days of life. If, in the first two months, the young animal is not in contact with, or receives little or no handing by, human beings, there is a strong tendency for it to grow up alienated towards the human family environment and everything contained within it. Naturally feral cats usually develop in this way; notice how a feral cat will run apprehensively off when you pause on a walk and say a few kind words to one that you meet. Say 'tch, tch, tch' to it and it reacts as if you are spitting fire.

Another important possible cause is poor parenting by the queen. If she, for whatever reason, perhaps inexperience or sheer ingrained incompetence, does not give her kittens the normal, invaluable, maternal attention and education we considered earlier, they can suffer for it. Of course, some individuals may be born congenitally nervous. As with us, where some people are, by nature, highly strung and what my grandmother called 'worrits', and others are placid and phlegmatic, so with cats.

Curing a fearful cat

How to cope with such a fearful feline? Simply wrenching it away from its hiding place and telling it to 'pull itself together' is utterly futile. Such an approach is likely to provoke an aggressive response in the shape of spitting, biting and clawing, and can only exacerbate the problem.

The younger the cat is, the better your chances of success. Approach the animal in a gentle, relaxed manner with abundant patience. Arrange regular sessions of acclimatization and familiarization, of simple friendship, where, at first, only you and the cat are together in a room. Try to initiate simple games like rolling balls of paper or pulling a small toy along on a piece of string. There should be constant, quiet talking and light stroking if and when possible. Food treats should be on hand. As things progress, other people and other objects might be introduced into the sessions, which can also, little by little, be held in other rooms. All this can take a long time to achieve results and most of the cats never lose all of their nervousness entirely, but if you can progress to the point where the pet only makes itself scarce when strangers ring the bell, it will be very well worth the effort. In severe cases, the process of slowly winkling the cat out of its timorous shell may be usefully assisted by the lightest doses of tranquillizers, such as Valium prescribed by a vet.

Xenophobic cats

Nothing is more enjoyable than visiting a home, particularly for the first time, and being welcomed by the family cat with affectionate rubs, purrs and, perhaps, soft vocalizations. Unfortunately, many, perhaps a majority of, cats are to some greater or lesser degree, xenophobic, fearing or, at least, disliking strangers if only for a short while. It may be fastidiousness or, perhaps more likely, the instinct handed down through generations of the family of cats, forged during millennia of ill treatment and even persecution at the hand of man. In some cases, a faulty kittenhood with insufficient contact with humans may be the prime cause; in others, some traumatic incident later in life may have been the deciding factor.

I experienced the stranger's eye view of cat xenophobia on innumerable occasions as a young vet in the days when house calls were, unlike now, routine, cheap and done at all hours and at weekends – even for hardly urgent cases of chronic skin disease. On so many occasions, I was met at the door by an apologetic owner saying, 'He went under the bed as soon as you knocked,' or, worse, 'He must be telepathic; can you get him out of the coal cellar?' My body still carries the scars of my subsequent attempts to get to grips with the patient. In extracting a Thinking Cat from his bolthole one has to try hard to out-think him.

Agoraphobic cats

One of the few true phobias of the domestic cat, and a rare one at that, is agoraphobia, the fear of open spaces outside the home. As I mentioned earlier, a form of agoraphobia can occur indoors with a pet being most disinclined to move away from cover while in a room. Although this is usually the result of lack of correct attention by the queen and/or human beings in early kittenhood, it may also sometimes be brought on by some alarming event or a change in circumstances out there.

It may be the arrival of a loud and aggressive dog next door, a warmongering un-neutered tom claiming the garden as its patch or the activities of noisy builders. The consequence can be that the cat chooses to stay indoors and protests energetically if it is forced to go outside by its owner.

Of course, if there is no other solution, a cat can – thousands of cats do – live a full life permanently indoors if it is provided with litter trays, toys and a range of spots where it can snooze or just sit and observe what is going on around it. But if a nice garden exists, why shouldn't the cat feel easy in using it?

The best way of dealing with cats whose agoraphobia is based on the possibility of bumping into enemies or other types of disturbing things or occurrences, is to erect a temporary pen of the totally enclosed, meshed variety widely used by cat breeders for queens to rear their litters in. The cat should be put inside the pen each day, at first for only a short time, but then gradually extending the length of its stay. It should receive its meals and be played with in the pen so that it associates it with pleasant happenings.

Eventually the cat can go outside into the garden without being put in the pen although, for a period of time, the latter should remain in place. The owner must always supervise these garden visits outside the pen, and it is ideal if the cat can be trained to go out on a lead (see page 150). A cat flap, if the pet knows how to use it, may serve as a useful escape hatch if anything does go amiss.

Treating the patient

Where the phobia is pronounced and every visitor is regarded as a clone of Darth Vader, patient treatment of the condition should be attempted. The aim is to put the cat into the presence of strangers without forcing it, so that it comes slowly to terms with them, accepts there is no danger and, basically, learns how to cope. The best way is to put your cat into a carrying basket with which he is familiar. With the cat inside the basket, place it in the room where you will be receiving your visitors well before the doorbell rings. It is a good idea for the first 'visitors' to be members of the family whom the cat knows well. When they enter the room, the cat, peering anxiously out of his basket, will recognize them and relax. The next stage is for 'real' visitors to come into the room. At first they can sit, talk, have a cup of tea, etc. but should not approach the basket or try to make any form of contact with its tense inhabitant. With luck, the cat, in the security of his container will gradually come to imagine that what seems to be OK with you, might be OK for him. Progress is made by repeated visits by strangers who, bit by bit, can sit ever closer to the basket, begin talking to him, and eventually proffer food treats through the mesh or grille.

In due course, and all of these stages must be reached very gradually over what often will turn out to be a very long time, you can arrange visits where the cat is out of the basket, held securely in your arms, ideally on a harness and lead, with the guest offering some tasty titbit to him on entering the room. The guest sits closer to you both now and can begin stroking gently the cat. Finally, as the guest strokes the cat and any tension of its muscles has gone, you can begin to move your hands away. Obviously, any sudden movements, loud noises or, yes, piercing looks into the cat's eyes, must be avoided at all costs. I repeat, making a xenophobic cat intruder-proof may well take many weeks, certainly not days.

Although they can be used, I do not usually recommend tranquillizers in cases of feline xenophobia, but there is no harm in owners trying floral essences or homeopathic remedies.

I have hand-raised a few big cat cubs over the years and have been involved with many more in the hands of clients. My experience has been, although my sample of cases is probably too limited in size, that xenophobia seldom develops, if at all, in them. It may be that the reason is the continual, intense human attention they receive. Whether this fits them for later life among their own kind is another matter.

The many faces of feline aggression

The two Kilkenny cats fought and fought until nothing was left of either animal except their tails.
Old Irish legend

Domestic cat aggression, for owners the most troubling of pet behaviours and potentially the most dangerous to the cat itself, comes in over a dozen distinct forms according to the cause. It can be directed at another cat or cats, at other animals, including prey, at owners and even at objects. The four main types of aggressive behaviour are:

■ Male-on-male aggression
■ Fear-provoked aggression
■ Territorial aggression
■ Competitive aggression.

Besides these, there is aggression based on predation, jealousy, play, mating, parental attitudes, petting by owners, pain and disease. It can be learned and also re-directed. Let us look at these in more detail together with possible ways of treating them.

Male-on-male aggression

This is the classic expression of feline machismo, battling sometimes, as it were, in a tournament with an audience, for the favours of a lady, or rather a queen in heat. A better comparison might be with Japanese sumo wrestling where much fearsome ritual is on display although, unlike in cat fighting,

Fear of prey

There are other kinds of fear, with which we shall deal presently, such as fear of an enemy, and there is also, on occasion, fear of prey. This latter phenomenon has been observed in both wild and domestic cats. A hunting cat may exhibit some signs of apprehension, even fear, for some time after tackling live prey. If, say, a threatened rat defends itself vigorously, the cat may in subsequent rat encounters, at least in the short term, behave in a wary, timorous manner.

rarely is any serious damage done. There is the unblinking, malevolent stare at the opponent, the raising of the hackles, the provocative body posture with arched back and ears standing out, and the accompanying vocals which, the contestants must hope, will curdle the blood – the menacing growls and the eerie caterwaul that sounds like a bad opera singer tuning up off key. The combat begins in slow motion, the pair prowling around one another before, again sumo-like, there is the sudden clash of bodies and the wrestling begins in earnest, bared teeth and extended claws brought into wicked play. There may be several 'rounds' in a fight with short intervals, but no water-bottle bearing seconds in between.

All this is normally, of course, the fault of testosterone egged on by ovaries in oestrus nearby, but it can sometimes take place between two neutered males. Some lines of cat (the samurai of the feline world?) seem to produce more and better fighters than others, but as well as skill in the martial arts being possibly inherited, upbringing and environmental factors can also influence the development of a warrior.

In cat society, particularly the feral community, battling is all part of the process of a tom holding on to its rung on the hierarchical ladder. The same jockeying for status through combat occurs in other wild cats, such as lions. Young, up-and-coming toms take on the older toughs. At first they may lose a series of contests, but usually, in the end, youth prevails. Faint feline hearts ne'er won fair ladies. Treatment for this problem, it goes without saying, is by castration. Administering progestagen contraceptive preparations can control serious fighting between neutered toms in a multi-cat household.

Fear-provoked aggression

As we have seen, in certain scaredy-cats, which are forcibly removed from their hiding places or compelled to go into a garden that holds unnamed terrors for them, an aggressive response might be forthcoming. Aggression is a very common reaction to fear in cats and it can happen in other circumstances to the above-mentioned, with far more distressing results.

'Fright, flight and fight', the famous trio of words that is well known to every student of physiology, indicates the phenomena associated with the fortifying surge of adrenalin into the bloodstream when danger threatens cat or man. When frightened, a cat may choose to flee – that's one of the strategies of the adrenalin-fuelled fright, flight, fight trio, and very sensible, too. Sometimes. however, there is no way out, the threat is immediate and present – the animal must fight defensively.

Defensive cat fighting differs in style from the offensive of the male-on-male 'arm wrestling' encounters, just as a boxer changes his fist positions and punching when under a hail of incoming blows. There is little or no use for the teeth, at least at first. Claws are the weapons for initial defence with the cat pulling in its head to protect the vulnerable neck and not trying to bite. Its body is flattened to the ground and the visible outline of its head is reduced by pressing the earflaps down and sideways. The pupils are open wide for maximum vision and the body hair bristles in order, perhaps, to make the defender look bigger. If the attack continues, the defender will usually roll over on its back but keep its hind legs firmly anchored on the ground. This gives the front half of the animal full freedom for the use of weaponry. Teeth now join front claws in punishing the aggressor.

Some cats, particularly those that have had long experience of human companionship, will try to get away unscathed (and often succeed) by doing nothing more than simply crouching, not moving a muscle and avoiding eye contact. I sometimes think they are trying to 'become invisible'. At the first available opportunity, often when the aggressor pauses or is distracted, the cat then slips away. Nevertheless, a display of apparent aggression by the defender, arching its back, increasing the effect by standing sideways on to the attacker, and hissing, perhaps then spitting, will often deter an attacker at the last moment. Cats tend to respect others that look as if they will stand and fight and will often decide to slope off when some young stripling of a fancy cat has the nerve to surprise them with a display that seems to say 'Come on then, let's be 'avin yer!'

Humans and dogs

Fear aggression is also used, as vets and owners know well, when the cat deems it necessary, against human beings and other animal species, particularly dogs. For cats a strategy where is the best means of defence pays dividends. Fleeing from a bothersome dog is likely to stimulate it to chase after the cat, regarding it as a prey animal running away. Even a small cat faced by a large dog will show some kind of aggressive defiance, facing up to the threat, standing its ground, back arched, hissing and spitting with gusto. This normally serves to give the irksome canid second thoughts. Aggression directed towards humans by fearful cats most commonly involves visits to the vet, cat-carrying baskets and car travel.

Causes of fear aggression

Fear aggression again is sometimes inherited from nervous parents, and upbringing and learning are important factors in the majority of cases. Some veterinary surgeons suspect that diet can play a part in feline aggression. As is known to be the case in some children, certain additives in prepared food may have an effect in stimulating a tendency to aggressive reaction. Giving fresh food, cooked chicken, boiled fish, boiled rice and the like, instead of tinned, foil-packaged or pelleted proprietary cat foods, could calm down certain individual animals.

Treating fear aggression

I have already dealt with treating cat basket and car trravel problems (see page 129). There is not much that one can do about the aggression evinced by the vet, his examination table and instruments. The vet must get by, bite and scratch wounds notwithstanding, as best he or she can. Some help in these circumstances may occasionally be called for in the form of a small dose of diazepam (Valium) or temazepam given before cat and vet square up to one another. Neutering does not affect fear aggression.

Territorial aggression

We have seen how territory – possessing ones own patch of land, part of a house, part of a room or, maybe, just a particular windowsill – is highly important to a cat's psyche. Intruders into such territory trigger an aggressive response from the 'property owner' in the form not of a no-trespassing injunction but of an immediate attack. Toms, curiously, may make it something of a bizarre, semi-erotic remonstration, attempting to mount the stranger, male or female, as if to mate with it. Sexual harassment of this kind is enough to put any cat off, and the invader will clear off post haste back to his own ground, often flinging out an indignant paw as it goes.

Sometimes, owners can also be treated as space invaders if they try to move a cat from its usual napping spot or while feeding. The offended animal may dispense a growl, even a lashing out, claws bared. Occasionally, after an established cat in a multi-cat household returns after spending time away from home, perhaps in a boarding cattery or veterinary hospital, it will be treated by the other cats as an interloper, just as if it were a new member of the family. This may be due to the unfamiliar smells it is carrying.

I have witnessed the same phenomenon in other species, with attacks being launched on the 'foreigner', the members of its pack, pride or herd, treating it as unrecognized even after a brief absence. A leopard, one of an established group of five animals, which had spent a week in a specialist veterinary unit after surgery on its cataracts, was bullied and abused by its companions of five years upon its return, as if they had never seen it before. I recall an Arabian oryx that I anaesthetized for emergency surgery in the Oman desert. When the knock-out drugs wore off and it, behaving as if nothing had happened, tried to rejoin its fellows who had been standing some distance away in the sand watching the proceedings, it was knocked about and treated as a most unwelcome outsider for some hours.

Treating the problem

Hormone or tranquillizer treatment is not of use in cases of territorial aggression, but castration may reduce it to a certain extent. As we shall see when discussing the arrival of new members into a family home, patient introduction and gradual familiarization of one animal with another are the keys to success. Each cat in a household should have some bit of space that it can call its own.

Competitive aggression

This type of aggressive behaviour is more subtle in some ways and less easy for an owner to identify. It consists of fighting between two individuals brought on by their hierarchical position combined with some act of competition. One cat that is, in the Cat Town or multi-cat household pecking order, above another and therefore dominant, may find its position relative to the other cat suddenly reversed if, in competing for some advantageous position, it loses out. For example, if, when trying to assert its generally accepted dominance, it attempts to 'lord it' over its inferior, perhaps approaching it with a cautious yet arrogant air and preparing to sniff its bottom, the other cat reacts by rejecting such familiarity, hisses or lashes out with a paw and jumps up onto some place above the sniffer, it becomes top dog – sorry, top cat – of the two. Its actions, especially its taking of a position above the other cat, make it now, at least in the short term, the dominant one. Re-matches of this scenario are likely to take place, with often more true fighting involved. The position of superior ranking can then swing to and fro between the contenders. It's a sort of game of the 'yah boo, I'm Numero Uno, so there!' sort.

Some experts recommend that owners who have cats that compete in this way should try to identify the one that is, by and large, the more naturally dominant and treat it in the household as Number One, the Alpha cat. With luck, the boss cat will then settle for nothing more than a token ritual demonstration of bravado, rather than actual scrapping, to maintain its position. I am not sure that this is always easy to achieve. In most cases, things sort themselves out and settle down quite naturally as the cats, without human help, organize their in-house social relationships.

Predation aggression

Naturally the cat out hunting for its lunch has to be aggressive. Predation is synonymous with aggression. A tiger mounting a ferocious attack on a buffalo is the epitome of naked aggression. For our pet cats, however, where meals come by room service out of a tin or packet, there is no call for aggression. Nevertheless, the aggressive hunter still lurks beneath the fur of the most domesticated, over-fed Puss, and modified forms of predation aggression, some associated with play, are to be commonly seen.

Kittens learn their hunting/killing techniques at first from their mother, and then, as they grow, refine them by continual practice. The skills they acquire are valuable in developing their judgement via their senses and the coordination of their senses with muscle action.

For the owner, the innate and learned hunting tendencies of their pet may be a worry if there are other potential prey animals, such as rabbits or budgerigars, in the household, but if a kitten is brought up with such creatures around and scolded whenever it makes a lip-smacking move in their direction, it eventually learns that they are not to be interfered with.

Dissuading a domestic cat, when outdoors, from stalking birds is more difficult. You may be able to apply a little aversion therapy by means of a water pistol, but are you always in the garden when the cat is? Belling the cat in the old-fashioned way may be all you can do, though I have known the occasional knowing moggy that somehow managed to muffle the bell on its collar (with a paw perhaps?) before making its final charge.

Some young cats treat parts of the human anatomy as substitute prey when playing, stalking and then pouncing on a foot or hand before biting it. It's all great fun – but it hurts. These cats need more to occupy their time and work off their enthusiasms – more playing with, more toys and items of interest and, best of all, more boxes of various sizes and shapes.

When they nip you, pick them up unceremoniously by the scruff of the neck, like their mother would do. Say 'No' firmly and loudly while looking them straight in the eye, and then put them down on the floor. Have nothing more to do with the rascals for five minutes. They will learn. Predation aggression is not affected by neutering.

Play aggression

Play aggression is just that: playing at being an aggressor, a predator, and it is an integral part of the feline character, as we have seen. Predation and play aggression merge into one another in the domestic cat.

When a cat catches a mouse and, before despatching it, plays with it and then later flings the corpse into the air or bats it around with a paw, it is re-creating what it loves about the hunt – the chase, the pursuit, the pounce, the movement. If it is a well-fed cat and doesn't eat the mouse, it soon loses interest in the immobile body. Pet cats are rather like foxhunters who claim in justification of their 'sport' that it's the riding they enjoy, not the murder of a fox. A lion would certainly not agree. Once adult, they, like other big cats, only hunt to fill their bellies, but there are other kinds of wild predator, such as the fox and killer whale, that go a-hunting sometimes just for the hell of it.

Jealousy

Any cat, not just green-eyed ones, can suffer from jealousy. They have emotions, and signs of jealousy can easily be brought on by the arrival of a new cat or person, often in the form of a baby, in the home, or the owner's apparently preferential treatment of one cat over another. One of my female Birmans thinks I belong to her alone and grumbles vocally and even half-heartedly strikes out with a paw, claws sheathed, if one of the others shows signs of jumping on my knee.

To express their envy, they may become tetchy and aggressive, taking it out on another cat or a human being, but they may elect to make their feelings evident by urinating in a strange spot or beating up the furniture.

Treating the problem

How to treat it? In many ways as you would a jealous friend. The most important aspect is to make the cat feel loved, wanted and holding an equally important place in your daily life as that of any other pet. Do all the things you did with him before the newcomer arrived, keeping to the old routines of feeding and play. As an established, 'senior' family member, feed him first. Make sure he has one or more elevated vantage points from which he can survey life in the house – a climbing frame, a ledge or shelf where he can perch, undisturbed, on high. Being up, looking down, always soothes the feline breast.

A new person in the house should not 'rush' the cat. They should speak gently, be patient, and let him make the first move. Gradually, as the days pass, they can begin to play with and give food titbits to the pet.

Where a cat's character seems to have changed abruptly or where he does not come to terms with the changed circumstances, despite all your efforts, it is wise to have the animal checked over by the vet in case some subtle underlying physical problem is masquerading as jealousy.

Mating and parental aggression

I have described the aggressive phases of male and female cats during the mating rituals (see page 59). Suffice it only to add that sometimes the repeated hard bites on the back of a queen's neck inflicted by toms can result in a temporarily inflamed and thickened area of the scruff. These 'love bites' rarely need medical attention.

The maternal instinct is exceedingly strong in most, but not all, queens. An alarm call from a kitten will bring an immediate response from not only the mother but also other queens in the vicinity. Woe betide any 'outsider'

New babies

These can often put a cat's nose out of joint. You should prepare the animal for the new arrival by accustoming him to the sight, sound and smell of all the nursery paraphernalia as early as possible. When the baby arrives, it is important to give extra attention to the cat, including when the infant is present. There is no harm at all in holding the baby in one arm while you fondle Puss with the other. Keep talking, whenever you have the opportunity, directly to your cat. In all cases the cat should always have somewhere, a quiet room ideally, to which he can retire and get away from any new form of bustle and busy-ness in the house when he wants to.

cat of either sex that has caused the call by nosing around, perhaps merely sniffing, the infant. The queen will go in, guns blazing. The worst cat fight I have ever seen was when a gentle, neutered cross-bred shorthair living in the same house just took a peep over the arm of a sofa at a pair of three-day-old Birman kittens in their nest on the floor. Golda, the mother, was transformed in the twinkling of an eye from her usual soft and placid self into a screaming, incandescent fury. She almost literally exploded as she attacked, every claw and every tooth bared and striking home. Humans can also be threatened on occasion if the queen considers them to be interfering with her young. The period of maternal aggression lasts normally for about three or four weeks after the birth of a litter.

Although, as we've seen, male lions often kill cubs sired by rival males, and the males of other wild felines, such as pumas, jaguars and ocelots, also occasionally indulge in infanticide, this is uncommon in domestic cats. There are cases where a tom will mistakenly try to mate with a young kitten having initially been attracted by the false heat of its mother that occurs while she is lactating, but found her unwilling to mate and positively aggressive. The death of the kitten comes about as the tom mounts it and, in the usual fashion, bites the back of the little animal's neck. A bite that would simply pinch the loose skin of a queen is lethal when applied to the entire, tiny, fragile neck of a youngster.

Very rarely, a queen will kill her own kittens, perhaps because the hormonal controls that inhibit her normally from regarding these small squeaking things as prey, fail for some reason. In male and female killings, instances of cannibalism have been recorded. It is likely that, where this occurs, it is not as a result of hunger, but the typical feline desire to keep the place clean and tidy, as well as an ancient instinct to remove anything that might attract scavengers to the nest.

Petting aggression

Petting aggression is typically seen when a cat that is, apparently, thoroughly enjoying lying on your lap being stroked, suddenly bites your hand or arm, jumps off and walks, always unhurriedly, away. I have one Birman, Sam, who does it fairly regularly. What have we done to deserve what is sometimes a very hard nip?

Cats, it seems, do not go in for lengthy grooming sessions among themselves. The main groomers are females and they only groom for relative short periods of time. Being so highly individualistic, cats do not want to be, as they see it, over-fussed by being stroked *ad infinitum*. It gets to the point where they become irritated and so demonstrate their irritation. Some animal behaviourists think it might also be due to them suddenly coming out of a doze and reacting automatically to something in contact with them before they realize that it's only you. They bite without thinking but then, finding it to be a false alarm, have the cheek to bear you no ill will! They will not mind at all if you reach down to stroke them straight away. Treatment of this form of fleeting aggression (which I keep forgetting to put into practice) is, of course, not to pet the cat for too long at any one time.

Learned aggression

Cats can learn how to be aggressive bu not, as is so often suggested to be the case with young people, by watching violent films on television or even David Attenborough's wonderful documentaries in which animal predators often display aggression of the highest order. (Although I do know a cat that sits transfixed before the screen when films of such things as cheetahs running or sea lions darting after fish are being shown.) Being intelligent and having a good memory, the Thinking Cat may find that acts of aggression seem to pay off. It can get away with things and control events by at least appearing to be aggressive to individuals of other species, principally man and the dog.

Where this is most commonly put into practice is with the family dog. The latter, so often a tolerate soul, puts up with teasing, paws in the face, even having its coat climbed up. It starts with the cat being brought up with the dog, quickly losing its initial fear and then finding that it can, in effect, rule the bigger animal by little displays of mock toughness. Of course, problems can arise if a visitor brings a strange dog along and the cat treats it without more ado in the same manner, assuming that all dogs are the same (and inferior). 'What the hell!' thinks the visiting labrador or terrier, rather taken aback when the resident cat calmly walks up and dings it on the ear. The dog snaps back.

Owners can be controlled likewise to do things that the cat wishes. This is usually to do with food. A nip of the hand or a quick paw at the leg of the human being will quickly bring the desired result for the cat – the opening the refrigerator door or the speeding up of dispensing the cat meat if the owner is daydreaming or talking on the phone.

How to treat this sort of presumptuous behaviour? Intervene. Use aversion therapy by reaching yet again for the water pistol or casting a pillow in the cat's direction when it occurs. If the importunate aggression is aimed at you, give the cat a bit of a scruffing, but do not reward it by giving the food or whatever it wants you to do.

Pain and disease aggression

Aggression arising from these causes is easy to understand. Tread on a cat's tail and it naturally reacts. Single incidents of that kind, I'm glad to say, are quickly forgiven and forgotten by the animal. No grudge will be borne – unless you keep on doing it. A cat will not punish its owner for taking it to the vet, once they are safely back home. With sick cats, aggression is just one of the behaviours that may be forthcoming as a result of not feeling well.

In old cats where joint pain caused by arthritis may exist, moving the animal may elicit an aggressive reaction. Cats with hypothyroidism, an underactive thyroid gland, may be irritable and short-fused. As I mentioned earlier, cats with rabies are frequently alarmingly and very dangerously aggressive. Tumours in the brain can have similar effects.

Of course, sick and off-colour cats will generally show changes in behaviour other than aggression. Apathy, dullness and inappetance commonly accompany feline ailments, from mild upsets of the stomach to more serious, perhaps life-threatening infections. The handling of all these requires early veterinary diagnosis and therapy.

Redirected aggression

This variety of aggression happens when the displeasure of the cat is vented on someone or something other than the actual cause of whatever has upset Puss. It may take place immediately or be deferred until a later time. The cat's motivation appears to be 'So you took me to that vet and had me pricked with a needle and embarrassed by having a thermometer stuck up my bum. Well, let me tell you, someone's gonna feel sorry!' The 'someone' might be a member of the household who had nothing whatever to do with the visit to the surgery. The mood of the cat in these circumstances has elements of fright and agitation within it, and tranquillizers such as Valium can be valuable in treating it.

4

Training the cat

It is a common misapprehension that cats cannot readily be trained. Not so. These intelligent animals can and indeed should be trained in certain basic behaviours which will make life both for the pet and the owner easier, safer and happier.

Training the cat... and how the cat trains you

Tearaway kitten or staid mother of fifty, Persian, Chinchilla, Siamese
Or backstreet brawler – you all have a tiger in your blood
And eyes opaque as the sacred mysteries.
C. Day Lewis, Cat

Your cat is trained in many ways by his mother when a kitten. Later come other things that your cat trains himself to do. He watches you and learns from observation – how to open a door, for example. Certain doorknobs or handles need a combination of manoeuvres by the human hand to make them function; a twist and then a pull maybe. The Thinking Cat watches and later, in its own good time, tries. Eventually, after experimenting with how and where to use its paws and the position and weight of its body, it succeeds. From then on, it remembers the technique. Refrigerator and room doors, drawers, curtains and blinds present no problems to the determined puss.

However, you have to train the cat in certain desirable respects, not to jump through hoops or 'die for the queen' (cats, being their own men, leave that sort of unnecessary display to down market, ever-eager-to-ingratiate dogs), but in useful, day-to-day, life-in-the family things.

As time goes by, although you may be the last to realize it, it will be you who is being trained, with your furry familiar as the trainer. It is done quite subtly, and older cats are especially good at it, most commonly when they have decided that a little reassurance and attention during the night would not be amiss. The artfully pitiful miaow, a voice of a quality that they reserve only for these occasions, is accompanied by that direct, unblinking, intense stare right at your eyes, when Puss would like you to open the door (often of the refrigerator), administer a cuddle or, a daily performance with my lot, move your bottom from the now-warmed cushion of the sofa so it can curl up there for a nap. You, like me, quickly become a biddable, house-trained pet, responding to the voice of your master or mistress. The odd thing is that, unlike the cat, as we shall see when discussing how to train it, we don't receive a reward for correctly and promptly performing our learned behaviours – no morsel of food, not even a 'thank you' miaow, and yet we still perform well. It looks as if cats are better trainers than us!

Training without coercion

Training, the modification of certain types of behaviour of an individual may, sadly, with some species at some times, involve cruelty. That is unacceptable and wrong. Domestic cats as pets, thank goodness, are only trained by kindness without compulsion – unless hunger is involved. While the vast majority of pet owners would never use food deprivation as a training tool, unfortunately certain professional domestic cat trainers for film and television commercials do. I know it from personal experience. Apart from the desire to eat, the cat's wonderful sense of 'self', of independent thought, does not permit coercion. Cats are not for pushing.

The same does not apply, more's the pity, to big cat training, or 'taming' as it is sometimes termed – a horrible word- in circuses, but only because the animals, free spirits as much as their domestic cousins given their liberty, can be coerced forcibly because of their close confinement with nowhere to flee to. Training methods of tigers, lions, pumas and leopards, as well as elephants, chimpanzees and bears, can be, and sometimes is, achieved by relatively humane methods of patience and reward, but often it is a regime infused with cruel practices. Having treated circus animals for many years, I now, because of that experience, unequivocally insist that these wild, exotic creatures ought not to be in the sawdust ring. Leave it to horses, dogs, maybe, and clowns.

Toilet matters: essential training

It matters very much what the Thinking Cat thinks about his lavatorial arrangements. Cats take such matters very seriously indeed. Clean and fastidious by nature and better brought up, some people may think, than most dogs, their sanitary facilities must be just so. This is, of course, especially important in those instances where the cat is not an indoor/outdoor one, but living permanently indoors in the house or apartment.

Litter trays

Owners must give careful thought to their pet's litter tray. It must be big enough and, if of the covered type, which is much preferred by the shier as well as many far less shy cats, the door must be big enough to allow the more portly puss to pass through. In multi-cat households, ideally there should be one tray per cat plus one extra. As with food bowls, cats don't relish queuing to use the bathroom.

Correct placing of the litter tray/trays is crucial. It should be in a quiet place off the main traffic routes through the house and, for older cats with creaking, arthritic joints, it may be easier for them if they don't have to climb stairs to use it. Keep the tray away from an area popular with a dog or used as a play zone by children. It should definitely not be near any feeding bowls. Cats understandably abhor using a loo sited next to their dinner plate.

They may also object to certain kinds of litter and to changes made in the type of litter. Refusal to use a litter tray may mean you are not cleaning the tray often enough for their feline sensibilities. Do not use strong-smelling disinfectants after cleaning a tray; some cats are put off by the odour. If it appears that a cat does not like a certain type of litter, experiment by putting down three or four trays with different sorts to see which it prefers to use.

Cats will use litter trays from an early age and are normally quick to learn. by following their mother, how to use them and where they are. The litter isn't just to absorb urine and coagulate droppings but also gives them that something they love instinctively to do after visiting it – scratching and raking. Very satisfying.

A young cat, newly arrived in a home, should be introduced at once to its litter tray and then watched carefully, particularly after waking, feeding and playing. Normally little training is required. At the first sign of crouching to pass urine or stools, pick up the cat and plonk it gently down on the litter. It will soon get the idea and recognize the smell of the litter as indicating its personal WC. Always praise the cat after a successful performance. I found this method worked just as well with twin orphan puma cubs that I raised at home. No more than one or two 'plonkings' were necessary before they became fully house-trained.

Wrong spots

A cat which urinates or defecates in the wrong place, particularly a formerly outdoor type who now must live indoors, can be taught by placing the litter tray on the spot it picked and then, after the animal has started to use it regularly, gradually moving it to a more desirable location. De-odorizing aerosols or mothballs can be used on the 'wrong' spots to deter repeat mishaps. The latter are especially good at stopping cats using houseplant pots instead of litter trays. Simply bury a mothball in the soil near the plant. Cats heartily dislike the smell and are most unlikely to try eating the mothball. Toilet 'accidents' were covered earlier (see page 118).

Using the lavatory

There is something of a vogue, particularly in the United States for training a pet cat to use the lavatory in the home, so dispensing with the need for a litter tray. I find myself ambivalent and slightly bemused on the subject. To train a cat in this way, the first step is to change the litter tray for an aluminium foil cooking tray of the same size. It is filled with litter as usual. The next step is gradually to move the foil tray closer and closer to the lavatory you plan to use. Don't rush; take a few days to do it. Once arrived at the loo, place the tray in the toilet bowl with the seat up so that it fits snugly into the aperture, bending over and moulding the rims of the foil sides so that the tray is held firmly in place when the seat is lowered upon it. For heavy cats, two trays forming a stronger double layer would be a sensible precaution; feline users have been known to plunge down into the toilet when the tray gave way. Not funny – at least not for the cat!

During the initial period of moving the tray, the cat will have been following and using it as necessary. When the tray is fitted to the toilet bowl, the cat must be encouraged to jump up to it by you scratching the litter to make the familiar sound and uttering encouraging remarks. It goes without saying that the toilet lid is left up at all times. With any luck, Puss will take well to the new positioning of its latrine and will use it efficiently.

Next, after about three or four weeks, begin reducing the amount of litter in the tray and make a small hole, about 2.5 cm (1 in) in diameter, in the centre of the tray. It is obviously advisable to use the biodegradable sort of litter that will flush easily away. From then onwards, the diameter of the hole is enlarged bit by bit by, say, 2.5 cm (1 in) per week. Again, don't rush what must be a steady, gradual process. As the hole increases in size, the cat, which began by squatting in the tray, will be compelled progressively to put more of its weight on the rim of the toilet seat. Eventually the stage is reached where there is no litter in the tray and the hole is so big that the cat is, more or less, using the lavatory like a sitting human being. The entire training time is usually between two and three months.

Overcoming problems

There are snags to the process. Young cats under about six months of age, probably because they are not yet experienced and skilled at balancing, take longer to train than old-timers. Also, there is no scratch-and-rake opportunity, so beloved by, and instinctive to, cats. The biggest problem is that cats cannot easily get a grip on the usually shiny wood or plastic toilet seat, and owners are advised to remedy this, and thereby avoid embarrassing, unexpected descents, bottom-first, into the bowl for their pets, by wrapping the seat in gauze bandage. The outcome of all this, as toilet- training owners freely admit, is that the lavatory cannot be used by both cats and human members of the family. So, in every house one bathroom is for the sole use of the Thinking Cat? The mind, excuse the pun, boggles.

Lead training the cat

Taking your cat out or a walk on a lead isn't quite like doing the same thing with a dog. Once you reach the park you won't normally be able to let it run free, for example, and cats object far more to rainy days than dogs. Most breeds of cat, particularly the Norwegian Forest, Maine Coon, Abyssinian, Russian Blue and the shorthairs, can be lead-trained. It obviously isn't so suitable for types like the Munchkin and Sphynx. Lead training is of value in exercising the cat and keeping it safe when you both go outside and especially if the cat accompanies you on holiday. However, you do need to begin early. Kittens take to a lead far more easily than older cats.

Wearing a harness

The first thing is to accustom the animal to wearing a chest harness. These can be purchased in the right size from pet shops. Eventually attaching the lead to such a harness is far preferable to using it on the collar. I don't like to see cats pulled by their necks, and anyway there is more control of the cat with a harness. Start by putting the harness on the cat and letting it wear it, no lead attached, around the house for short periods at first of five or ten minutes' duration. Gradually increase the length of the harness periods until you reach the point where it happily wears the contraption all day long.

Next, attach the lead to the harness. You should use a special light cat lead, not the heavier sort that is suitable for dogs. Again, let the cat wander around trailing the lead, without you holding on to the other end, for longer and longer periods. It is important to keep an eye on the cat during this stage of familiarization in case the lead gets snagged on some item of furniture. When the cat reaches the point where it is happy to trundle about your home, totally unfazed by its harness and trailing lead, you can begin going for walks together indoors.

Walks and car travel

Finally, when the cat does not pull back or otherwise object to you leading it about in this manner, you can begin to venture out of doors. Make short trips at first, always accompanied by frequent words of encouragement. Be ready, if there is any possibility of coming across a dog, to gather up the cat and hug it to you until the threat has passed by.

The harness and lead are also very useful when accustoming a cat to travel by car. They can travel without these devices, but in the early stages, there is a serious risk of a cat moving in a panic around the inside of the vehicle, interfering with the driver and causing an accident. You can't depress the brake pedal if a cat is cowering beneath it. (It's happened to me.) If a cat is to become a seasoned, carefree car passenger, it is vital to start as a kitten. Another person, besides the driver, should always be in the car to control the cat. That is where the harness and lead can assist matters. After a number of short journeys by car, a young cat will normally adapt well to this method of transport and become rather fond of going out with its owner while comfortably stretched out on the back window ledge and enjoying watching the world speed by. A few cats, far fewer than among dogs, are prone to travel sickness when taken out in the car. The symptoms of impending trouble are restlessness and salivation followed eventually by vomiting. Tranquillizers and anti-emetic tablets can be obtained from the vet to prevent this occurring in cats that are known to be susceptible to motion sickness.

Basic training

The very first 'training', if you can call it that, which a kitten receives after the teaching given by its mother, is when it arrives in a family and learns to be sociable. It requires virtually no effort on your part. The animal has to be talked to, stroked, yes fussed over, by human beings, as many as possible, and also introduced to others of its own kind. The crucial time for acquiring these social graces is between around three and twelve weeks of age.

Another kind of elementary training is accustoming the cat to being handled in certain ways. By regularly doing things like opening the mouth, inspecting the ears and unsheathing and examining each claw in turn, you will make things so much easier for yourself and your pet if it has to receive veterinary attention or have its nails clipped or ear drops applied at

Learning its name

The cat must learn its own name. We can put aside, for the moment, T.S Eliot's insistence in The Naming of Cats that a cat must have three different names! Again, this comes naturally if you say the word at the same time as it is experiencing something pleasurable, a sort of reward it can associate with the name, like food or fondling. Very quickly it will respond by looking at, or actually coming to, you when you say its name. By looking at the cat, touching it in some way or giving something directly to it, each youngster in a multi-cat household soon learns to whom you are referring.

any time in the future. In addition, you may spot the development of something undesirable in its very earliest stages. Although cats, by nature, are more resistant to being trained in many ways than dogs, horses or dolphins, training must be done with abundant patience and understanding on your part. Young cats under six years of age are the best for training.

General training principles

These are the same as those that are used with other species: no punishment, no coercion, but rather training by reward, positive reinforcement as it is called, together with a bridging signal. In a nutshell, this is the reinforcement of the idea in the cat's mind that it has just done something correctly and of which you approve, by giving it a reward at the same time as you give a signal, usually a word or sound, that will bridge cause and effect, stimulating it to link performance and reward mentally. It is vitally important to establish the link in the feline mind that you are extremely prompt in giving the reward, which may be a food titbit, or playing a game or receiving a caress. Undoubtedly, a tasty morsel is the most popular feline reward item. Chunks of the cat's regular proprietary cat food are not regarded as a reward. Something more glamorous must be thought of, such as prawns, pieces of smoked salmon or a favourite cheese perhaps. However, some cat experts have demonstrated that certain behaviours can be trained solely by use of the voice without food reward; we'll deal with that later in relation to problem correcting.

Speed is best

While there must be minimum delay in presenting the reward, the bridging signal that indicates successful accomplishment can also give you a little time, as the cat will take the sound as a promise of the goodies that are imminently on their way. I have met many would-be animal trainers who were not very good at their job simply because their reactions were not sufficiently sharp; they did not 'bridge' quickly enough. This is not so much of a problem with cats as with, say, dolphins. The latter do things, correctly or incorrectly, at a very high speed, and trainers need to be ultra-fast in informing the animal that it has done well by means of the signal, usually in their case, a whistle.

Clicker or voice training

As the training of proceeds, the sound of the voice may be a reward in itself for the cat. Most owners clearly will use the voice, a word of praise, as the bridging signal but some, particularly those going in for more advanced training, prefer to employ a clicker, a small plastic device held between finger and thumb. Clicker or voice training is not time-consuming; sessions of up to five minutes, no more than three times a day, are enough.

Whether your training objective is to get the cat to come to you, to sit or lie down, the basic procedure is as follows. By clicking (one click will be enough) and giving a food titbit without the cat having done anything, you will create the association between the sound and the reward. This must be repeated many times.

■ Click and reward only when the cat has done something you want it to do. Give a verbal cue in advance to indicate that you are about to reward if the cat does whatever you want it to. This cue acts, in addition, as the command word or words, and the cat soon learns to recognize the meaning of 'Sit', 'Come here' or whatever it is you are training. The animal is studying English! After successful completion, click.

■ If the cat nearly, but not quite, does the correct thing, still reward and click. This encourages the animal to progress in the right direction.

■ For specific actions that you want to train, use food in the hand as a magnet. By holding it just above his head and slowly moving it back towards the tail, the cat will tend to go into a sitting position. When it does, reward and click. By moving your food-bearing hand down between his forelegs so that his head follows it, and then very slowly withdrawing it towards you, the cat will crouch forwards and, with any luck, lie down. Reward and click.

You will need to practise and refine the hand movements that do the trick with your particular puss. Once the cat is sitting or lying, the click and reward can be delayed for a few seconds at first, and then gradually for longer and longer, until you have the cat trained to sit or lie for extended periods of time. Of course, throughout all this, the cat will be thinking that he, by doing certain things, is training you to click and give treats. Eventually the food in the hand and the hand movements will no longer be necessary, and if you have also been giving verbal cues along with the clicker you will be able to discontinue using the latter.

The same system with clicker or verbal signals can be used to train the cat to come to you. Sit on the floor some distance from the cat, pat the floor in front of you and say, in an encouraging tone of voice, something like 'Here, Mephistopheles, that's a good boy.' When he makes a move in the right direction, click and reward. Repeat frequently until perfect.

Intermittent reward system

When the cat's training is well advanced it is not necessary to give a food reward after each correctly accomplished behaviour. You can begin to reward intermittently. This tends to strengthen and lengthen the desired behaviours. If, however, the intermittent reward system breaks down, go back to rewarding every time and then try again rewarding intermittently at a later date.

Training is fun

These training sessions should be conducted in a quiet part of the house with just you and the cat in attendance. A training session works best, as if you haven't guessed, when a cat is hungry, so don't forget to have a plentiful bowl of suitable titbits in there with you. Using the above methods, virtually any owner can train his cat into a small repertoire of behaviours. Some of them may hardly be necessary to a successful cat/owner partnership, but they are fun, strengthen the bond between man and animal and, importantly, keep the Thinking Cat's mind active.

The initial repertoire might well comprise behaviours such as 'Come', 'Stay', 'Sit', 'Jump up here', 'Give me a paw', and 'Give me the other paw'. Training can serve even more useful purposes. A recent development in America is the training of Hearing Ear cats. As well as giving their deaf owners companionship and affection, these talented animals indicate by paw tapping or some other behaviour that the telephone is ringing or there is a knock at the door.

Cat flap training

I should mention one other important area of training for a cat: the use of that invaluable device, the cat flap. When first presented with one of these, most cats are nonplussed and need to be shown how it works.

Don't try to push the cat through the flap; doing so can produce feelings of aversion and he may avoid it at all costs from then on. Start off by leaving the flap fully open, secured by a piece of string or sticky tape. Entice the cat to come in rather than out with the aid of some favourite food or an intriguing toy. By this means you will set up an association between the flap, the reward and the warmth and comfort of indoors. Once the cat is passing through repeatedly without any apparent worries, begin to lower the flap very slowly over several days. Puss will become accustomed to having to push, at first a little and then a bit more, to gain entrance. However long it takes, you must not get exasperated and lose patience. All cats eventually use their cat flaps satisfactorily. Some individuals learn the knack far quicker than others, and in a multi-cat household the animal that learns first how to do it is normally copied very rapidly by all the others.

Dissuasive training

Finally, we must not forget what I term dissuasive training: teaching the cat not to do certain things like scratching the furniture or nipping your flesh with its teeth. The signal and 'punishment' for such misdemeanours may be a quick squirt from a water pistol or the noise from shaking a can of coins in the case of the furniture scratcher and a loud cry of 'AOW!' to admonish the nipper. They soon get the message. I will deal with this problem in more detail later (see page 173). Consistency is essential. You, and all other human members of the household, must always react in the same way when what you all agree are 'bad' undesirable behaviours occur. Conversely, you should always give praise for 'good' behaviour.

Cats and their home

A home, be it a den, nest or a house or apartment shared with humans, is the nucleus of a cat's life. It is the centre of its territory although, if it is a multi-cat household, the cat may 'own' only part of the dwelling. Cats are, if you will excuse the expression, 'home birds'. They seldom leave their home base for long voluntarily, even if they are badly treated by man or beast.

Cats on the move

Moving house is a traumatic experience, for cats no less than owners. The owner usually is looking forward with pleasant anticipation to the new abode, a fulfilment perhaps of years of planning and saving. The cat, highly attached to its territory, has no such sentiment, and, as we have seen, may try to find its way back there, given the chance. Home to a cat is a place, a geographical point that happens also to be inhabited, sometimes by other familiar animals, and certainly by humans of which it is quite fond. However, it is the place that counts to the cat with family coming second. For you and me, the reverse is normally true.

Planning ahead

Moving the cat to a new house requires some planning. It cannot be sent in the pantechnicon with the Welsh dresser and grand piano. The best arrangement, if possible, is for the animal to stay in the old home until the new home is basically ready for occupation, removal men gone, carpets down and furniture in place, but not necessarily before all painting and decorating (which, as we all know to our sorrow, can take months!) is completed. If the cat cannot be left in the old house, boarding it temporarily with a neighbour or in a cattery are the best alternatives. Before the cat does arrive on what will be his new territory, check to make sure there are no open windows in the attic or gaps in the floorboards.

Settling in

When, at last, Puss moves in, he must be kept strictly indoors for at least two weeks. If there is still much moving about and commotion in the house, it is wisest to confine the cat to one room. As things settle down, he can be let out to explore one room at a time, best of all with you as guide and mentor. Thought must be given as to the positioning of food and water bowls and litter trays in the sort of 'cat friendly' locations I mentioned earlier. Put the cat's bedding down in a quiet, snug place that seems likely to meet with his approval; you'll probably get it wrong, but that's cats for you! Wherever possible, bring things like the cat's bed, bedding, litter tray and other utensils that carry the animal's own scent from the old home.

When you do eventually start letting the cat go outside into the garden, it should be for no more than about thirty minutes at a time to begin with, always under your supervision and, most importantly, when the cat is hungry. Have his favourite platter ready for him when he comes in.

At about the same time, you can begin letting him use the cat flap, again under supervision, and with the lock set at the 'entry only' position at first. Naturally, the cat must always be back safely indoors, with the cat flap locked, by nightfall.

New animals in the home

Bringing a new cat into a household where there are already one or more resident established felines or a dog can understandably present problems, but they are not insurmountable. Much depends on the age, breed and individual character of each of the animals involved. Among cats, shorthairs are the friendliest with strange cats, while Siamese and Burmese and, to some extent, Abyssinians are the most xenophobic. Old cats are more tolerant than young ones of other established cats in the family but they take longer to adapt to the arrival of new youngsters and will express their displeasure with more episodes of hissing, spitting and paw batting than younger adults.

Old timers, on the other hand, accept kittens, with better grace than other adults. Although the boisterous little tearaways will pester the veteran for games just when he feels like yet another nap, there is no competition between them, and the old cat, wiser and more experienced, feels in control of things in general. Young adult cats adapt better to the introduction of new young adults. However, old cats put up fairly easily with the arrival of other old cats if there are enough snug sleeping places, observation perches, food dishes, litter trays and individual fuss from owners to go round everyone.

A cat of either sex can be successfully integrated into a multi-cat household, provided it has been neutered. It would be ridiculous to bring an un-castrated adult tom into a family with other cats even if all of them were already neutered.

Introducing dogs and cats

With dogs being introduced to cats or having cats introduced to dogs, the breed, character, and experience of the canine individual are of the utmost importance. Some dog breeds are not easily introduced into a family with a pre-existing cat or cats, particularly if they have not been brought up with cats. Greyhounds, other breeds of hound, terriers, particularly the Jack Russell, and, sometimes, German Shepherds and the collies, can be dangerous and impossible to mix with cats if they have never had the experience of living with them peaceably. It's in their nature to chase after smaller, fast-running creatures. Labradors, spaniels and toy dogs are far easier to bring into feline company. Gentle, placid, lazy characters get on better with cats than active, bustling, wilful ones.

It is vital to know all the details of a dog's past history and character before considering it for introduction into a cat-containing house. The same considerations apply, of course, if you are thinking of bringing a cat into a house where a dog already lives. It is clearly an advantage if the cat involved in these amalgamations is also experienced in living with dogs. A new cat brought into a home with more than one dog is especially vulnerable. Being, by nature, pack animals, a multiplicity of dogs is much more likely to persecute a cat than one on its own.

Introducing cats to cats

The key requirements in bringing a new cat into your home where another cat or cats are already well established are patience and a gradual approach. First, allow the newcomer to explore the house without coming into any contact with the feline inhabitants. The reason for this is that behaviourists have found that where a cat is on unfamiliar territory and meets a strange cat which is familiar with it, the former is far more interested in first investigating its surroundings than in checking out the other animal. As I said earlier, territory is of supreme importance to cats

Next, put the new cat in a room alone with its own food and water bowls, litter tray and bed. Begin feeding the new cat and the other cats on either side of the door, putting their dishes near, but not too close, to the door. Gradually, over a day or two, move the dishes closer to the door.

Now, open the door a crack, just sufficiently for the cats to be able to see one another while they feed, and wedge it. Also, exchange the bedding of the newcomer and the residents so that they become familiar with each other's scent. Some experts actually recommend spraying both lots of bedding with one of the cat scent pheromones, such as Feliway, that are now available. Once the newcomer is eating and using its litter tray regularly, allow it out from time to time to explore the house again, still without meeting the other cats face to face.

Finally, you can open the door wide for a while so that the cats can mix. Do it gradually, extending the contact time more and more as things settle down. There may well be some moderate displays of aggression and fear with some growling, hissing and spitting at first, but unless they are severe, these almost always tend to diminish steadily. If you see either cat becoming distinctly aggressive or frightened, separate them, not by charging in but by throwing a large towel over each of them and carting them off so that they can reconsider things. You will then need to begin the introduction process once again. Make sure you have a litter box for each cat plus one extra. During the 'getting to know you' period, which can last weeks, it is best to keep the cats separated when you go out.

Throughout the process of introduction, it is vital that you continually boost the confidence of the resident cat. It should receive more attention, more fussing over, than the new arrival. Of the two cats, it is the one to feel affronted, and it will be on the lookout for any sign that your affections have been transferred to this Johnny-come-lately. Of course you must make friends yourself with the newcomer, play with it, stroke it and talk to it, but in the initial period you should do this only when the resident cat is not present. Whenever you are with the cats, keep talking, always quietly in an upbeat, encouraging tone of voice, never shouting or scolding.

This familiarization by separation technique, of introducing animal strangers to one another is essentially the same as that used in zoos and safari parks for tigers. In their case there is more visual contact, as the two animals are on each side of a gated mesh barrier. There is of course no question of human beings going in with them, let alone holding them on laps. With tigers, the two individuals get to know one another well, but without bodily contact, over a much longer introductory period of at least one year. When, at last, it is considered time to open the gate and let them mix, it is always an event of high tension for the zoo staff, even though for months the animals may have behaved impeccably towards one another.

A tranquillizing dart rifle is loaded and ready, just in case, although most tiger introductions pass off without trouble, but it is not very uncommon, as the two big cats at last come face to face with no weld-mesh between them, for one suddenly to pounce and, within the twinkling of an eye, deliver the classical, lethal neck bite. No time for tranquillizing darts then. The cause of the tragedy, once again, is probably territorial.

Introducing cats to dogs

The same system can be used with cats and dogs, but after a week or so of eating at opposite sides of the door, a face to face meeting, with the dog on a lead, in the same room, can take place. Make sure the dog obeys its commands to 'Sit', 'Stay', etc., and have the two animals at first on opposite sides of the room with the cat held on somebody's lap. Titbits should be proffered all round. This scenario should be repeated many times until there is no sign of aggression or fear from either party, the cat in particular not struggling to get away. Then the two animals can *slowly* and progressively over a number of meetings be brought closer to one another. The dog should be praised and rewarded for good, obedient behaviour in

Additional considerations

When introducing a cat into a household in which a dog is already resident, you should bear the following considerations in mind:

■ *The cat must have escape routes and sanctuaries in the house available at all times. Faced with a bothersome dog, a cat's first reaction is to flee and hide rather than make a fight of it.*

■ *When you are away from home during the introductory period, you should always keep the two animals separate.*

■ *Always feed the cat on a shelf or a working surface – somewhere high that the dog cannot reach. As ever, a high vantage point will give the cat a feeling of security and contentment.*

■ *Place the cat's litter tray somewhere where it can gain access, but the dog cannot. Keep the cat flap locked until peace and amity reign in order to deter the cat from leaving home for good.*

■ *Feed the dog separately and alone; dog food is not suitable for cats and a cat trying to take a mouthful from the dog's bowl could cause the dog to react tetchily.*

■ *Until the dog is totally unconcerned by the presence of the cat, you should leave its lead attached to its collar, even in the house, just in case it decides to make a dash for Puss and you have to grab it.*

■ *It is sometimes worthwhile giving the cat and the dog each its own territory; for example, the cat having upstairs and the dog downstairs. There should be no trespassing, to begin with at least.*

■ *Don't rush things. Remember that the introduction period between the two species can be as long as three months or even longer.*

the presence of the cat, never punished, so that it does not come to regard the cat as being the cause of any punishment. That could lead to the dog 'taking it out' on the cat when it got the chance.

The next stage is for you to arrange scenarios where the dog and cat meet in the same room with the door closed. Don't rush bringing the two together; let them take their time. The dog must be watched carefully and on its best behaviour, calm and obedient, with no excited prancing about or barking. You will need patience as the scenario will have to be repeated perhaps many times, but eventually the two pets will metaphorically shake hands, or paws, and become friends.

Aggression in the home

All cats, whether Siamese, snow leopard or alley cat, are essentially solitary beings with a highly developed sense of territoriality. Put a number of them together in a household and, if it is done sensitively by the owner in the way we have just discussed, a happy family of humans and moggies can be established. But there is no such thing for man or beast as a state of everlasting bliss. Times change, accidents happen and every living thing gradually gets older. So, as in all societies, stresses and strains may arise from time to time showing themselves as spats, altercations and alterations in particular relationships. Some are short lasting and over in minutes or hours, but others may be more permanent. Among the cats of a multi-cat household these strains are manifested as aggression at some level, and the precise causes of the strains can be several.

The demise of the Godfather

Old cats may, as the years pass, lose their status in the family hierarchy. They take things easier as they age, becoming less competitive and more interested in the creature comforts of life, like a warm bed in a spot that they can call their own and regular meals of a favourite food delivered by room service. The other cats recognize that the former Top Cat is now retired and they are happy to leave him alone in possession of his small territory without let or hindrance.

Sometimes, however, the old timer is not ready to relinquish his position as chairman of the board, and aggressive confrontations may take place when younger members insist upon him standing down. Old cats can end up getting bullied by others who sense their failing faculties, particularly if they become ill.

161

Illness, and perhaps degenerative changes in the old body alone, cause alterations in the identifying scent of the individual. The familiarity and sharply defined recognition of the veteran are weakened and, in consequence, cats that have lived amicably together, perhaps even being related, may grow apart and the young may show antipathy or seeming contempt towards the old.

What determines the strength and durability of relationships among the household cats can depend on genetic factors – friendly parents produce friendly kittens; on kittenhood experience of socializing – happy, unhappy or absent; and on the lifestyle of the cat as a young adult – a cat who lived on the street and survived by its wits and claws, battling for territory and a square meal, will adapt less well to the 'soft' life in the home than one that has known nothing but human care and attention, perhaps even being born in the very house it now lives in.

Oi! Why did you just clip my ear?

Redirected aggression is targeted on some individual or object that is not the actual cause of the aggressor's displeasure or fear. It is very much a case of 'I'm hitting you because he upset me.' A typical example is a cat sitting looking out of a window when an 'outsider' cat calmly strolls across the garden, invading owned territory. What a liberty! Trouble is, the offended cat is indoors and can't get out to deal with the miscreant, so it attacks another of the family cats sitting nearby, treating it as a sort of enemy by proxy.

This rather unfair dispensing of retribution can also happen very suddenly if a cat is startled by something. In a flash, without thinking, the Thinking Cat will lash out at the nearest available animal. A cat on the receiving end of such undeserved treatment may forgive and forget almost immediately – after all, it has perhaps lived peaceably with the aggressor for many years – but, more often, days or weeks will pass by before relations get back to normal. Worst of all, a vicious circle of bad blood can develop between the animals, with initially re-directed aggression leading to defensive aggression that then triggers more aggression and so on indefinitely.

Trespassers will be prosecuted

Aggression among family cats is most often essentially all about territory within the house. Both males and females can become highly proprietorial over 'their' sleeping place (by day), sleeping place (by night), observation/vantage point and even a whole area of the building or garden, chasing away, hissing at and swatting any trespassers. Territorial disputes most often occur when a new cat arrives in the house, when a kitten reaches puberty and wants its own bit of space or when a resident meets up with an 'outsider' cat in the garden, yard or anywhere out of doors claimed as belonging to it by right. Cats of either sex, neutered or un-neutered, can display this sort of aggression.

Tom trouble

Male cats do tend to fight with other males. Un-neutered toms, as you might expect, are the worst for this, particularly if there are un-neutered females to impress. They are also more likely to scrap for hierarchical reasons, attempting to climb higher up the not very stable ladder of social status and dominance in the feline branch of the household, but neutered toms will sometimes do this, too.

Self defence

Fear-provoked aggression, or defensive aggression as behaviourists call it, is, in my view, a glaring misnomer. The dictionary defines aggression as 'an unprovoked attack'. Quite. Defending yourself, reacting to a threat, is prudent self-interest, not pre-emptive bellicosity. A cat displaying this so-called 'defensive' type of aggression is merely seeking to protect itself against an imminently anticipated attack. Adopting the typical posture, crouching with legs withdrawn under the body, tail tucked in and ears laid back, will be seen in the home when the cat feels frightened, threatened by another cat or the owner, or, sadly, after punishment by an owner.

Handling aggression between cats

The first thing is to separate the warring factions to allow tempers to cool down. It may be necessary to put each cat in a room on its own, with food, water and a litter tray for a few days, while you develop a re-education programme. No cat should be allowed a free run of the house during this time, but you should spend some time with each on a regular basis, talking to it, playing with and handling it. After four or five days 'in solitary', you can begin to let one cat at a time out into the house alone, at first for a short period and then, over the next days, gradually extend it. When both cats appear to have settled down, they can be let out together for 'association periods', under your supervision, and again for gradually lengthening stretches of time. Any sign of renewed hostilities and it's back to the slammer and start again!

When the cats are together you should feed them and give them favourite titbits. In this way, they will come, hopefully, to associate pleasure with the presence of the erstwhile foe. The rewards will act as positive reinforcement for civilized behaviour. If, however you rush the re-introduction process and insist on mixing the cats before signs of aggression have disappeared, the rewards may work in the opposite way by reinforcing the bad behaviour.

Things to avoid

■ Do not allow a fight to continue. Put a stop to it by throwing a towel or blanket over them or a soft cushion at them, startling them by making a loud noise or squirting them with water.

■ Do not wade in and try to prise the fighters apart. You may get badly injured.

■ Do not administer any kind of physical punishment. To do so could easily trigger further aggression with the other cat being blamed for your actions (a form of re-directed aggression) or you could become the target for fear-provoked aggression.

■ During the re-education period, it may be advisable in some cases to use tranquillizing medication as prescribed by your vet. Certainly the cat pheromone vaporizers, such as Feliway, that plug into an electric socket are worth using day and night in rooms where the cats are.

Cats and humans: problems of co-existence

Human beings and cats: two species of very different type. One is a big omnivore of a generally gregarious nature, with a primate physique originally designed for life in the trees, but now, in the majority of individuals, out of shape and clearly incapable of swinging from any sort of branch. The other is a small hunting predator, solitary and independent by nature, with an athletic physique that is mostly kept in well-tuned condition.

Throughout history they have been associated in many ways, most of them lamentable, but now, in the twenty-first century, the picture for the pair is much

> ## Social anxiety
>
> *At Cornell University in New York, veterinary researchers are developing a drug, clomipramine, which is used in humans to treat panic and anxiety attacks, for use on aggressive, bullying felines. The scientists believe that some the violent behaviour of some moggies is rooted in a condition of 'social anxiety' and this type of anti-anxiety therapy may well prove to be very effective.*

rosier. In the United States and Great Britain, cats have become more popular as pets than dogs. They have the advantages of being self-exercising, easy to house and cheap to feed. (My wife has just muttered something like 'You and your five Birmans and their *a la carte* tastes! Cheap?')

They are good, faithful companions, ideal for the elderly or infirm, and make an elegant and decorative addition to any home. Only once have I been called to a tiger, an adult, being kept as a pet in an ordinary house. The owner was a stage magician living in a bungalow near Dumbarton in Scotland, the tiger having one bedroom to itself. That sort of pet-keeping seldom occurs nowadays. The Dangerous Wild Animals Act has very wisely put a clamp on it. I wonder how the ancient Egyptians went about keeping big cats around the place. Very recently, a mummified lion, bred in captivity, and a creature considered in those days, like the domestic cat, to be a god, was found in the tomb of King Tutankhamen's wet nurse in Saqqara.

Introducing new human members of the household

The two creatures, man and cat, living under one roof, can, like any cohabitants, have their differences of opinion and disagreements from time to time. Let's have a look at them. I have already dealt with the owner's handling of a cat when a new baby arrives in the home but more briefly with the cat's attitude to new adult members. It's worth going into a little more detail.

The cat, understandably, will view the newcomer first and foremost as a big, two-legged competitor for your affections. It will immediately spot who now gets greeted first when you come home, and who gets fuss and attention for some time before you seem to have time to address Puss. What is more, the newcomer may well be sleeping in your bed and occupying the space that rightfully belongs to the cat or, what a nerve, actually taking over a favourite napping spot on a particular chair standing just to the right of the fireplace. Rather 'put out' to say the least, Puss indicates his displeasure by growling whenever the person enters the room and, quite frequently, urinating on the bedspread or, even more wickedly, on the trousers or skirt of the interloper.

What to do? It's all down to the newcomer. As ever, the pathway to a cat's affections passes through its stomach and the problem human should do all the feeding. He or she should stay in the room while the cat feeds, at first well away from the affronted but eating feline, and preferably sitting on a chair or, best, on the floor so as not to look 'so big'.

Steady talking is invaluable in such circumstances: quiet, friendly words, but without looking directly into the cat's eyes. Take your time; don't 'push' the cat – it will not respond well to forced introductions. It can be useful to put one of the newcomer's items of unwashed underwear near the cat's food dish or on its favourite sleeping place. Scent, and familiarization with it, are as we have seen, very important in the feline world.

Cats and babies

As a boy I well remember old people telling grim tales of how cats smothered babies in their prams or cots by lying across their faces, attracted by the smell of milk. Nobody, it seemed to me then, had actually witnessed such a tragic event, nor did they know chapter and verse of a single proven case, but it is, at least theoretically, a possibility. The belief in the danger posed by cats to infants is still around today, and it is certainly important to ensure that a baby is never left alone anywhere where a cat might try to use an infant as a comfortable, warm cushion on which to curl up. A pram net should always protect a baby sleeping in its pram outdoors.

When the child becomes a toddler, it is the cat who may well need the protection from rough handling, so again no young child should be left unsupervised where a cat is present, particularly if it has no escape route.

Aggression towards people

We have already discussed the various kinds of feline aggression, some of which can occasionally be directed at human beings. Owners can find themselves the targets of fear-provoked, territorial, predation, redirected, petting or play aggression after having a role in some aspect of the aggression's cause. With most of these forms of behaviour the signs of a cat being in an aggressive frame of mind are obvious to the owner. With petting aggression, however, there are some warning signals that indicate the cat is beginning to lose patience with you and is likely to bite at any moment. These are: the cat's tail beginning to twitch, the onset of restlessness, the ears turning back or flicking to and fro, and, most commonly, the cat turning or moving its head towards your hand. Suffice it for me to reiterate three points.

■ Do not try to handle a frightened or aggressive cat; you could get badly bitten or scratched.

■ Never administer punishment; it will only make things worse.

■ If a problem with aggression is severe, prolonged or recurring, seek help from your veterinary surgeon or an animal behaviourist.

Very occasionally when a frightened and aggressive cat is holed up in some fairly inaccessible place, a vet may have to use a tranquillizing dart fired from a silent blowpipe. I have been called out a few times over the years by local practitioners to do just that. It made a change from firing through letter-boxes at drug dealers' pit bull guard dogs during a police raid or, as in Holland in 1983, through a window we had had to break to capture an escaped orang-outan that had taken refuge in a zoo restaurant.

Feeding problems with Puss

Cats can go off their food for all sorts of reasons. Some of these are physical, like tooth or gum trouble or being ill in some way, and these naturally require veterinary attention. However, there are times when even perfectly healthy cats refuse to eat.

Sad cats

Cats suffering from some form of anxiety, such as grieving over the death of a much-loved companion, human or feline, can go on a sort of hunger strike. These cases need plenty of care and attention. Where possible, the cause of the anxiety can be tackled or a bereaved cat can be much helped by the acquisition of a new kitten. A variety of tasty food titbits may tempt the animal. Food can be gently warmed before setting down, thereby releasing appetizing aromas, and liquid or semi-liquid item, like Complan invalid food, beef tea, or meaty or fishy baby food, often work. You can try hand feeding or increasing the fat content of the food by mixing in a little warmed beef lard. Make sure the food is properly seasoned with salt, as you would for yourself. Most cats approve of a light touch of garlic in their grub, too. Like many vets, I have found that the best dish for getting a sad or convalescent cat eating is tinned sardines or pilchards in tomato sauce.

In appropriate cases, a veterinary surgeon may prescribe anti-anxiety drugs or appetite-stimulating anabolic steroids, the same substances that hit the headlines when professional sportsmen test positive for them. I wonder if one of these days we'll hear a famous athlete or footballer defend himself by saying, 'My coach mixed up my vitamin pills with the ones he was giving to his skinny cat.' It could end up being a contest between a moggy and an Olympic gold medal!

Fussy cats

Then there is the mighty constituency of pet cats who are just fussy, spoilt and faddy. They have their particular likes. Trouble is, the particular like can often change by the day. If the owner does not cater precisely to the particular like, the cat intimates that it will starve itself to death. It never does, of course, not least because the owner fears that it might, and hurries off without delay to obtain what it is hoped might be that day's particular like. Here again we have an example of the Thinking Cat cleverly training the owner to do his bidding.

What is the answer? Either, like me I must confess, you accept your role as cat- servant and continue buying a multitude of mouth-watering (you hope) offerings and then depositing them in the waste bin the next morning, or you adopt an air of steely resolve, put down one good variety of balanced and fully supplemented cat food, and refuse adamantly to change to another brand. The cat will eventually knuckle under. So they say: easier said than done.

One-track appetite

More importantly, there is the cat that insists on eating only one kind of food; something that is not a balanced preparation. From time to time I have come across cats that will only partake of freshly poached plaice (off the bone, of course) or Welsh lamb's (most certainly not beef) liver. Such restricted fussiness leads to health problems. A diet of nothing but white fish can result in Vitamin B1 deficiency, while nothing but liver can produce skeletal disease because of excessive intake of Vitamin A. If a cat is on a regime of nothing but raw minced meat, it is not getting the calcium and other minerals it needs and is, no matter that the mince is bought from a reputable butcher, at some risk of contracting infections such as Salmonella. The owner must address this by very gradually mixing other balanced foods of the proprietary tinned, semi-moist or dry sort, into the cat's meals.

Dining out

One thing to bear in mind when a cat either doesn't eat or eats very little is that it might be dining out. It is well known that some cats with access to outdoors pop along regularly to a neighbour who, perhaps believing that the dissembling moggy has no home to go to and is desperate for a crust, provides excellent home-cooked dishes on the kitchen windowsill.

Oysters and caviare

Talking of restricted diets, it is fascinating to note that Dr Samuel Johnson's cat, Hodge, was fed on a diet purely of oysters. These molluscs were very cheap, indeed the food of the poor, in eighteenth-century England. In the United States in the 1930s, caviare was a common free nibble, a fore-runner of today's peanuts, provided by bars to encourage patrons to drink, and cats belonging to the establishments would frequently be seen feasting on these fish eggs de luxe. On the subject of caviare, last year a talented cat in Russia named Rusik, with a nose as good as that of a bloodhound, who was used by police to sniff out hidden consignments of caviare and sturgeon fish being illegally taken out of the country, was deliberately run down and killed by smugglers driving a van in which he had just located some of the fishy contraband. On very rare occasions I've tried my Birmans on a bit of fresh oyster, always to their disgust and provoking much shaking of paws. I have never offered them caviare yet, but they are equally unimpressed by lumpfish roe.

Fat cats and thin cats

Over the year, a cat's weight waxes and wanes. This is quite normal although science cannot yet explain why. At the point in this cycle of gain and loss where the weight starts to fall, the owner may note a marked reduction in the cat's appetite or even a short period of total inappetance.

Cats that eat too much may be suffering from a medical condition, such as some form of anaemia, an over-active thyroid gland, diabetes or, in rare cases, a tumour in the brain. However, there are some animals that compulsively overeat for non-medical reasons and the majority of them live permanently indoors. The cause can be boredom, with not enough in their environment to stimulate, occupy or amuse them, or stress of some sort, perhaps competition with other cats or a dog in the household, or a constantly noisy environment.

Preventing obesity

The Thinking Cat by nature is slim and trim and, left to itself, it would not get fat. Where a cat does overeat, and there is no medical abnormality or the use of drugs like Valium that have appetite-stimulating side-effects, involved, it is the fault of human beings – how we house, maintain and provide sustenance for our pets.

When the first signs of obesity become evident, it is important to cut out treats, give only two meals a day, and increase the fibre content of the food – easily done by adding bran or a breakfast cereal such as All-Bran. Recent work by pet food nutritionists suggests that even better is the so-called 'Catkins Diet' comprising high protein and low carbohydrate (including low fibre) and sold commercially as Prescription Diets. The cat's weight should be monitored weekly. Dieting an obese cat should only be done under the supervision of a veterinary surgeon. Too precipitous a drop in weight can result in liver trouble.

Strange food

Pica, the scientific name for depraved appetite, does occur in cats. I have described earlier how some animals will chew and then swallow plastic, rubber or fabric of various kinds. (I must say they are never as bad as walruses I know who will literally eat anything, and have a particular taste for coins, polythene and epoxy resin.) The cure for this lies in aversion therapy – applying deterrents such as eucalyptus oil or bitter lemon to the materials – together with diversion of the cat's attentions to play or time spent outdoors.

Among the strange things which I have known cats to love eating, and which don't appear to have done them any harm, are popcorn, vanilla ice cream, jalapeno peppers, ladies' hand cream and coffee grounds. What did do a cat considerable harm was eating a quantity of marijuana resin which a hippie, high himself on the stuff, had foolishly given it. (Yes, it was in the days of Flower Power, Janis Joplin and all that.) The poor animal, semi-conscious and seemingly hallucinating, had to be hospitalized for five days and only just pulled through.

Wool eating

This is one of the commonest and least understood of strange appetites in the cat. Although swallowed wool can pass through the digestive tract and be deposited in the faeces without any untoward effect, sometimes obstruction of the stomach or intestine by masses of wool occurs, with serious consequences that usually necessitate surgical intervention.

Wool eating is not an indication of some nutritional deficiency, although increasing the amount of fibre, such as bran, in the diet or converting to dry food is, in some instances, beneficial. Stress, such as moving house, may be a contributory factor, and researchers have found that it commonly begins within a month of entering the new abode. Other theories postulate that wool eating is related to the comfort-seeking kittenhood behaviour of sucking on the mother cat. Perhaps such cats still have an infantile aspect to their behaviour, and so should be helped to 'grow up', not least by reducing the amount of fussing bestowed upon them by the owner.

Treatment consists of denying access to woollen objects, applying nasty-tasting substances, such as cayenne pepper, to them, and, in the case of indoor cats that seem especially prone to wool eating, encouraging them to go out more. Some behaviourists consider wool eating to be an expression of the instinct to hunt fur-covered prey animals. Their recommendation for treatment is to supply the cat with gristly meat and meaty bones to chew, as substitutes for small mammals.

I have only ever met one big cat that was a confirmed wool eater. A lion, it would occasionally manage to hook the scarf or hat of a visitor pressed close to its cage on a claw slipped neatly between the bars. Retrieving the garment, it would then happily munch and consume the whole of it, never, I'm glad to say, with any ill effects except once, on a Bank Holiday, when a hat pin transfixed its upper lip and I had to sedate it to remove the offending article.

Cat alone

One cat, one owner, living together in a house or apartment. Sometimes problems can arise when the owner is out at work all day and the cat comes to resent being left alone for too long. I know many cats in that position which cope very well with eight or ten hours' minding the premises by themselves. Some breeds are better at it than others. The Devon and Cornish Rex and Persians seem to be able to occupy their time more satisfactorily than Siamese and Burmese.

A cat that is resentful of being left for long can express its feelings in one of two main ways. It may appear depressed, being less active and playful when the owner is around, and perhaps eating and drinking less than before. Another cat may become excessively demanding, constantly pestering for attention and miaowing more or less non-stop as soon as soon as it hears the key turn in the lock.

Treating the problem

One obvious solution to the problem is to provide the pet with company in the shape of another cat. If this is not desirable or possible, then it is essential with both kinds of behaviour to provide lots of toys and diversions in the form of boxes, climbing frames or play stations. Leaving the television or radio on all day does seem to be a good idea for at least some cats. However, with the attention-demanding type, especially one which in former times perhaps enjoyed your presence or that of some other person for longer, or throughout the whole day, you have to gently teach the animal to be more independent so that it can cope without you.

The best way of doing this is to have intense play and fuss sessions with the cat shortly after you return home. Ten or fifteen minutes are long enough. After that, for a further thirty minutes or so, have absolutely nothing to do with the cat. Do not talk to, touch or even look at it. If it jumps up on your lap, remove it gently without saying a word. After the half hour is up, you can revert to normal interaction, neither over- nor under-doing it.

For the first week or so the cat may seem to become even more insistent and importuning, but before long it will get the idea. There are focused fun and attention times for you both and times when you each do your own thing. It is surprising how quickly the penny drops in the Thinking Cat's mind after the first few days.

Behaviour in the house

The Cat, if you but singe her Tabby Skin,
The Chimney keeps, and sits content within;
But once grown sleek, will from her Corner run,
Sport with her Tail and wanton in the Sun; She licks her fair round
*   Face, and frisks abroad*
To show her Furr, and to be catterwaw'd.
Alexander Pope: The Wife of Bath her Prologue, from Chaucer

In Britain when cat owners get together, the topic of their conversation, after the weather, is certain to be the doings of their pets, particularly doings they cannot quite understand. Nowadays there is a growing number of animal psychologists available for consultation, and one can foresee the time when a feline annexe is added to The Priory clinic and anger management seminars will be organized by the Department of the Environment for un-neutered tomcats. In the United States, astrologers have been around for years who claim to sort out pets' problems by studying their star signs, assuming you know the exact time of birth of the troubled Puss, and marriage bureaux for lonely cats are not difficult to find.

Questions and answers

The most frequent behavioural oddities of our domestic cats are usually discussed with friends, veterinarians and breeders. Let's take a look at some of these now in question and answer form.

Q *Why does my cat scratch the furniture and how do I stop it?*
A Cats scratch, as we have seen, to leave territorial markers and to tidy up the old, outer layers of the claws. Scratching also exercises the muscles and tendons of the forelegs. It is a natural behaviour and, ideally, is only performed outdoors, but indoors it doesn't take long for your precious eighteenth-century writing desk or Shaker chair to be seriously damaged. Where a cat scratches in several different places in the house, it may well be influenced by psychological factors, such as insecurity and low-grade stress involving contentious territorial rights, brought on, for example, by the arrival of a new cat in the household or the visits of outsider toms who come spraying doorsteps or window frames. Cats

173

Scratching posts

Scratching posts or boards covered in rope, coarse hessian material or similar fabric, some impregnated with catnip, are available at pet shops. Some posts form part of a pre-fabricated play structure that also carries toys helping to attract the cat. It is vital that the post stands firmly and does not wobble in any way. Place it at first near to the area being scratched and, when the cat is using it regularly, gradually move it to some more convenient spot. When the cat uses the post, congratulate it and, in the early days, give it the occasional small treat, thereby positively reinforcing the behaviour. Multi-cat households need more than one scratching post, although any one post will often be used by several animals.

motivated purely by the claw-tidying desire tend to scratch only in one place. The insecure cat picks scratching places that are usually on their territorial boundaries like doors and windows.

Treatment is never by physical punishment; it would be ineffective anyway. A little aversion stimulation in the form of a water spray or loud noise when you see the perpetrator about to go into action is acceptable and can be useful. Covering a scratching area temporarily in tin foil or double-sided sticky tape often deters scratching; applying a proprietary deterrent aerosol spray or citrus oil, the odour and taste of which cats detest, will have a similar effect.

For the insecure scratching cat, reassurance is most important. It should receive plenty of fuss and attention and be handled as outlined for occasions when there are newcomers to the family. Places where outsider cats are spraying should be cleaned thoroughly with warm water and detergent and then have some citrus oil applied.

Q *When my cat is on my lap why does it sometimes knead or bite me?*
A Kneading with the front paws, usually of the owner's stomach, is an expression of affection. It is a throwback to the cat's kitten days when it lay against its mother's warm body and kneaded her mammary glands to stimulate 'let down' of the milk supply – a pleasurable experience which it

recalls instinctively when enjoying being with you, its friend. Some cats dribble while on their owner's lap. Again, this is an involuntary expression of happiness and contentment with echoes in the cat's mind of how, getting ready to suckle from its mother, its saliva began to flow in anticipation.

I have dealt with biting that occurs in similar circumstances under Petting Aggression (see page 142). Kittens have teething periods between the ages of three weeks and six months during which they naturally need to bite and chew on things. Give them small toys or bits of the cow leather dog chews sold in pet shops. They should be trained by encouragement to bite these and warned off human body parts. When a cat does bite, you should show it the error of its ways immediately, not by slapping it, but by scruffing it or, very effective, blowing hard in its face. It will soon learn not to do so.

Q *Why does my cat often paw at the window or inside of the bath?*

A Your cat does this because of what it can see. In the former case, there is something outside the window that interests it and, not understanding the physics of transparent objects, the cat is trying to go and have a look. The shiny surfaces of most baths give a faint reflection which is seen far more distinctly by the powerful eyes of the cat. It begins to paw and scratch at the moving image of a feline that, without emitting any scent, is clawing back at it. This phenomenon is puzzling but entertaining for the cat, I suppose.

Q *Why does my cat often put a small toy or stolen sock or similar object in its food or water bowl?*

A This is a behaviour that is based on the ancient lifestyle of the cat family. Wild cats bring dead prey back to their lair or nest; hunting domestic cats often come home with a dead mouse or frog. The nest, the home – these are the safe, secure points in their territory. A domestic cat that does not or cannot go out hunting still has the powerful feline hunting urge which it displays when it stalks, chases after and pounces on toys, pieces of paper or balls of wool in play. In the home, particularly in a multi-cat household, it may not have one particular nest, so it instinctively takes its 'prey' to the place that is at the centre of its daily life – the food or water bowl – and deposits it there. It is not, as my wife believes our cat Muffin is thinking when he drops paper balls into his water bowl on most days of the week, giving it a drink!

Q *Why has my cat started to howl during the night?*

A The night-time yell of a cat, one of the most distinctive of the sixteen vocalizations that behaviourists recognize in the species, is something that most often starts to occur as the cat gets older. These strident calls – summons would be a better word – are at first less commonly emitted during daylight hours. It's all to do with the senior catizen feeling in need of a little reassurance and attention now that the nights of searching for a way out of the house to go clubbing in Cat Town are long gone. More and more it appreciates the value and companionship of its human friends so, in the still of the night, it calls out for them. Up you get to see what is amiss and find the cat sitting there, cool as a cucumber, with no sign of trouble in the offing. A pick-up, a cuddle, a stroke and a few words of affection and you pop him back in his sleeping place. All is well.

Of course, some cats prefer the added sense of security of sleeping on the owner's bed and will yell again to make the point. Once curled up on the eiderdown, the cat doesn't move till your alarm clock goes off. All of this is training – the cat training you. It quickly learns that the yell evokes an immediate response and so, as time passes, is gratified to find it can get the owner to come running whenever it cannot decide whether to sit in front of the electric fire or on the mantelpiece. The owner's fussing, which involves making the yeller comfortable in one of the two places, or on an even better third location, proves it. The cat eventually has the owner perfectly conditioned to the point where the yell will work at any time of day or night. It is easier for an elderly animal to do than using energy going to find the owner and jumping up on their lap or tapping them pitifully with a paw.

Much younger cats sometimes go in for night yelling. Again, the cause is normally a feeling of insecurity and anxiety after some change in their environment, such as moving house. The cat is calling for reassurance. If it persists for long after whatever change in circumstances triggered it, the cat has learned that it now has a way of demanding the owner's attention. Whilst I would recommend tolerant acceptance of this behaviour in a venerable cat, I think it is important to try to eradicate it in younger exponents of the yell. To do this you must have an iron will, and ignore the attention-seeking vocalizations. Combined with this, aversion treatment administered via a squirt from a water pistol or a sharp noise as soon as the yell begins is very effective. After but a few nighttime yells more, peace will descend once again upon the sleeping household.

Q *Which kind of litter is best for my cat?*

A This all depends on the cat. It may prefer and, in some cases, agree to use only one of the various available kinds. These are the Fuller's earth, the clumping, and the biodegradable wood pellet types. The clumping one is lighter, longer lasting and very economical, while the wood pellet one is flushable down the toilet, unlike the other two. Cats like to use sand best of all – like their African wildcat ancestors. For the domestic cat, however, sand has its drawbacks, not least in being light and powdery and easily scattered out of the litter tray by the cat's post-toilet scratching. It is worth noting that in homes where children have a sand pit in the garden, it is not unknown for the pet cat to decide to use that as a toilet in preference to its own tray. There are health risks for the child, and pregnant mums, in this. Parasitic worms and, more importantly, toxoplasma germs can be left in the sand by the cat's droppings. If you have a cat and a sand pit, cover the latter with some form of protective sheet when it is not in use.

Q *My cat seems to be losing its 'house training' and has begun spraying indoors. Why?*

A Faults in toilet behaviour and the phenomenon of spraying indoors were discussed earlier beginning on page 117.

Q *My cat has begun biting one of its paws repeatedly to the point of drawing blood. What is the cause of this?*

A I discussed obsessive-compulsive behavioural disorders earlier on page 96. This kind of self-damaging obsession, along with chewing, licking or pawing to an excessive degree, is really a more extreme version of over-grooming. It is very worrying for the owner, and usually indicates, in the absence of any form of irritating skin disease that might provoke the biting, that the cat is undergoing some form of severe and ongoing stress in its life. Often it is very difficult to pinpoint the causal stress. Fortunately, such conditions are very uncommon, but there is no doubt that veterinary attention is called for at once. Sedatives, such as Valium or psychology-modifying drugs, given for at least a short time, may well be indicated here.

Q *My cat eats grass and plant leaves. Why does he do it, and is it OK?*

A Cats, both domestic and wild, as we saw earlier, do take some vegetable matter in their diet occasionally. Pet cats will chew grass and other plants and this may give them certain trace elements and vitamins that they instinctively need to obtain. Grass eating may also have an emetic effect helping them to regurgitate furballs.

Plant eating is virtually impossible to stop and, unless the plants are poisonous or valued by the human members of the family, not really of any consequence. Eating grass does not cause furballs, but may help them to be regurgitated from the stomach which is all to the good; they are better out than in. If it involves Aunt Matilda's beloved pot of orchids, there is nothing much you can do except move the plant to somewhere hopefully inaccessible to Puss. With permanently indoor cats it is worth buying one of the grass seed trays specially sold for cats at pet shops.

Q *My cat is always catching and eating flies. Will this harm him?*
A No, almost certainly not. The risk of picking up disease from a swallowed fly is very small indeed. Fly catching is just another aspect of the cat's hunting instinct.

Q *Can my cat read my mind?*
A Lots of people think so, and there does seem good reason to believe that telepathy of some kind exists between cats and their owners. Dr Rupert Sheldrake has done work on this recently and he found that many cat owners believe their cats can sense when a visit to the vet's is due. All but one of the vets in north London that he surveyed said folk often cancelled their appointments because they couldn't find the patient. The one other vet had stopped taking cat appointments because there were so many 'no show's. There is a wealth of anecdotal evidence that cats can anticipate their owners arriving home, even in an unfamiliar vehicle, at an unscheduled time and, most surprising of all, up to ten minutes before they walk in the door. Acute hearing and the recognition of car engine sounds cannot explain that.

Q *Can cats swim?*
A Yes, they can if they have to but, except for the Turkish Van which enjoys taking a dip and swims rather well, they aren't very good at it. Most of the wild cats, including the lion, tiger, jaguar and leopard, are good, even strong, swimmers. The Fishing cat, as befits his name and staple diet, is a most capable diver and swimmer. All cats swim using, yes you've guessed it, the dog paddle.

Q *My pedigree un-neutered queen was caught by a wandering local tom while she was on heat and went on to present us with a litter of charming but mongrel kittens. Is she now useless for breeding pedigrees?*

A This is a surprisingly common misconception among owners of dogs as well as cats. Having had cross-bred kittens cannot affect the purity of the pedigree of any future litters when she is mated with a male of her own breed.

Q *Is it true that the Ragdoll cat is insensitive to pain?*

A Absolutely not. This is a myth that has grown up around this delightful breed.

Q *My cat likes gardening, at least where it involves him digging up my bulbs. How do I stop him?*

A Repellent sprays and granules are available from pet shops. You could also try putting down pieces of lemon peel near the bulbs. Placing chicken wire flat on the soil will allow plants to grow through the mesh but will deter cats, who generally dislike walking on it. When you see the cat about to start gardening, a squirt from a water bottle or turning on the sprinkler can be used as negative reinforcement to make your point.

Posionous plants

Some plants that you may have in your house or garden are poisonous for cats which nibble them. Do not allow plant-chewing characters access to the following:

- *Tree lovers (Philodendron sp.)*
- *Dumb canes (Dieffenbachia sp.)*
- *True ivies (Hedera sp.)*
- *Elephant's Ears (Caladium sp.)*
- *Poinsettia (Euphorbia pulcherrima)*
- *False Jerusalem cherry (Solanum capiscastrum)*
- *Oleander sp.*
- *Rhododendrons and Azaleas (Rhododendron sp.)*
- *Common or cherry laurel (Prunus laurocherasus)*
- *Mistletoe.*

Q *We are over-run by mice. Would keeping our cat on short rations make it a better mouser?*

A No. Some domestic cats are just naturally better at catching and hunting mice than others. They don't do it for food because they are hungry but for their deeply ingrained love of, and skills at, hunting. A well-fed cat is at least as good at mousing, and arguably better, than one with a rumbling tummy.

Q *My tomcat was neutered a little while ago, but he is still spraying and even tried to mount my un-neutered queen when she was on heat. When will he stop doing such things?*

A It all depends on the age at which the cat was castrated and how long ago is 'a little while'. If he was castrated as a mature adult, he may continue with his old macho behaviour, including fighting as well as the things you mention, for several months after the surgery, but it will eventually subside, though some residual sexual interest in queens on heat may remain virtually indefinitely. A tom castrated before sexual maturity would not behave like that.

Q *Is it a good idea to take our cat on holiday with us?*

A It all depends. If the cat is a seasoned traveller and can be relied upon not to wander off from the holiday residence very far, or is happy to remain all the time indoors with a litter tray, food, water and all the usual mod cons of a cat, you can do it; some folk take their cats away regularly, more often to a rented villa or cottage than to a hotel. Obviously there is some risk. Taking a cat abroad – and it is done- means not only coping with road and sea or air travel, but also arranging the Pet Passport needed for it to leave and return to the UK without being quarantined. Rabies vaccination, rabies blood testing and veterinary certificates will also be required. Travel overseas carries a small, but significant, risk of contracting one of the exotic cat diseases not found in Britain. For me, the best thing for a cat when you go on holiday is for it to stay at home under the care of a daily cat visitor or sitter. Second best is to put it in a boarding cattery or take it to a friend's house – provided there is no chance of it escaping.

Q *Which is the most intelligent breed of cat?*

A It is impossible to say, though I am sure Siamese owners would insist it is the Siamese, Abyssinian owners would claim the Number One spot for Abyssinians, and I, naturally, would plump for Birmans. Tests, such as those recently carried out on dogs and which found Border collies to have the highest IQ and Afghan hounds the lowest, cannot easily be applied to cats. Working on the proven biological principle of hybrid vigour, however, I am strongly of the opinion that the cats with the highest intelligence quotients will be cross-breds, good old common-or-garden, but wonderful, mongrel moggies.

Q *It is sometimes said that too much red meat, at least in humans, increases the tendency to aggressiveness. Is that the case with cats and could I help curb my cat's fighting urge by giving more starchy food like rice in his meals?*

A Some scientists think, though it has yet to be proved, that a high-protein diet has the reverse effect of that you mention. High protein is known to increase the levels of a chemical called serotonin in the brain and one of the effects of serotonin is to inhibit aggression. So could it be that a diet that was 100 per cent meat, chicken or fish could calm a cat down? We don't know. Certainly a permanent diet of nothing but meat or fish, raw or cooked, will eventually produce signs of malnutrition in the animal, because of its insufficient content of minerals and vitamins. All proprietary cat foods are nutritionally balanced but hardly any can be considered high protein.

Q *My cat appears to sulk whenever he does something wrong and I reprimand him. Am I imagining it?*

A A cat that has been 'told off' does not sulk in the strict sense of becoming sullen and resentful, but it can sometimes look as if it is walking away from you and sitting down with its back to you, seemingly unwilling to look you in the eye. To cats and some other species of animal, a direct look, an unblinking stare, is a confrontational, challenging, often threatening signal. What the cat is doing when it 'sulks' is actually accepting the situation, acknowledging the reprimand, and not wishing to take matters any further. Good cat.

Q *Why are cats such enthusiasts for boxes?*

A It is probably because of the cat's essential character which was handed down from its wild ancestors. Wild cats of all species have their nest or den, the core of their territory where they can rest up, sometimes eat and usually give birth to their young. To the independent-minded and individualistic cat, these places are quiet and secure havens after a day or night out hunting. For the domestic cat, which is influenced by the ancient ways of jungle, savannah or mountainside life, boxes can take the place of those wild dens.

Q *My cat flicks and whisks his tail a lot. Is he continually angry?*

A Cats do swish their tails when cross or going into battle, but another, more common, reason for it is a sign of indecision. Most times when your cat flicks his tail it's the same as you pouting your lips or furrowing your brow when you aren't sure what to do next.

Q *Why does my cat indulge in a 'mad dash' around the house from time to time?*

A 'Mad dashes' in our house often seem to take place at about five or six o'clock in the morning. A not-so-subtle wake-up call? No, this is just the cat releasing excess energy. It's one of the ways, stretching is another, by which cats, far more than dogs, keep themselves in trim even when confined mainly or completely indoors.

Q *Why does my cat continually scratch wallpaper?*

A For the same reasons that they scratch furniture, which we discussed earlier (see page 173). Some cats seem also to do it for the pure enjoyment of feeling their claws raking through the texture of the paper.

Q *How does my cat recognize me – by my face, my voice or my smell?*

A By all three. First, it recognizes you by your unique facial features and voice, and then, when you are closer, by your smell. It can also identify a familiar gait. Cats greet any animal, even if it's the first time of meeting, by cautiously poking forwards, eyes scrutinizing and nose sniffing. If there is the slightest hint of a threatening signal, by sound or by posture, the cat will go instantly into defensive battle mode. Any movement by smaller animals is taken to indicate that they are prey, and the cat will adopt its hunting 'crouch, stalk, lying ready to pounce' routine.

If neither threat nor prey is identified, the cat will begin the usual friendly 'how are you?' ritual of rubbing and gentle bumping with raised tail. Behaviourists believe that people are treated in the same way as if they were cats, and that much of a pet's behaviour is most easily interpreted with the owner in the role of just another moggy. It has often been recorded that where a cat has been, for some reason, without food for three or four days, it will go through the polite, amiable greeting routine with a human before tucking into the food that has been brought, and the very hungry creature is desperate for. What exquisite feline manners!

Q Does the domestic cat ever mate with wild cat species to produce hybrids?

A Yes, but this happens very rarely, and perhaps only in special circumstances. The Bengal breed of cat, which has been around for only some twenty-five years, is the one definite example. It was developed in the 1970s in the United States by crossing domestic shorthairs with tamed, captive Asiatic leopard cats from south Asia. The Bengals of today are only six or seven generations removed from their truly wild forebears.

More doubtful, but a distinct possibility, is the mating of a domestic cat with a Scottish wild cat, without any human involvement in the process, to produce the so-called Kellas cat, a large, black, ferocious-looking creature that does not resemble any feline known to science. This mysterious creature was first brought to public attention in 1984 as inhabiting the remote Kellas forest in the Scottish Highlands. There have been a few reports of it since then, but its true nature, whether it is a hybrid or just an unusual melanistic form of the Scottish wild cat, is a matter of continuing scientific debate.

Q But wasn't that beautiful spotted breed of cat, the Ocicat, which resembles in some ways wild cats like the ocelot and margay, also developed from domestic cat/wild cat cross-breeding?

A No. The beautiful Ocicat was actually developed from crosses between three domestic breeds: the Siamese, Abyssinian and American shorthair.

Q Why does my cat insist on removing food from his bowl and eating it on the floor?

A Not because cats are untidy, far from it. It is because food on the floor is easier to break up into smaller, easier-chewed pieces than food in the bowl and also, maybe, because cats do not like the sensation of their whiskers touching the sides of their bowl as they eat. To prevent your cat doing this, why not try chopping up the food before serving it on a bigger, shallower dish?

Q *My cat is very timid and hides away much of the time. What can I do?*

A As with people, so with cats. Some individuals are extrovert and outgoing; others are of a more nervous and withdrawn disposition. A timid cat that hides away may just be happiest much of the time curled up in the security and privacy of its nesting place, which is often under a bed or in some dark cupboard. That sort of pet should be allowed to take life at its own pace and come out as and when it feels inclined. If, however, it has started hiding due to some frightening incident, such as being harassed by children or repeated loud noises, it is up to you to help improve matters. Stopping whatever it was that initiated the fear is the first thing. Then, with patience, the cat should be encouraged, when it comes out for food, by being petted very gently, without any pushiness on your part, talked to quietly and supplied with treats. It is wise for just one person, a calm individual, adult or older child, to do all of its feeding so that it can latch on to someone it associates with positive, pleasant things It should never be dragged out from its hiding place and compelled to join the family, let alone be punished in any way. It could be worthwhile giving the cat Rescue Remedy, one of the Bach's Flower Essence preparations.

Q *A neighbour's cat has apparently run away. Why do cats sometimes do that?*

A The commonest reason for a cat running away is after moving house. These highly territorial animals try to get back to their old stamping grounds. That is why a cat that is moved to a new house should be kept indoors for at least two weeks, and then gradually let out under supervision and just before mealtimes so that it will be keen to return inside when it has exercised.

Permanently indoor cats disappear sometimes when a door or a window is accidentally left open. Inquisitive about the world out there, they leave the house only to find themselves in strange, foreign territory. Scared, they then hole up somewhere and can get locked in, say, a neighbour's garage, or may actually be too frightened by their experience to come out, even when their searching owner calls for them. This is commoner with timid-natured cats.

A third reason, of course, is a sick or injured cat, which is frightened by what it is feeling and is seeking somewhere, anywhere, under cover to hide away, hoping, I suppose, that the pain will pass off.

Very few cats run away from home because they have been ill-treated. To cats, it seems, home territory outweighs home unhappiness. Sadly, the idea that putting butter on a cat's paws prevents it from straying is an old wives' tale.

Q *What are the objections to the de-clawing of cats, which is still legal in the USA?*

A De-clawing is a surgical operation performed under general anaesthetic to remove the nail and first joint of each toe. The purpose is not for the cat's health and welfare but, mainly, for the health and welfare of furniture and wallpaper. The operation is associated with post-operative pain, which has to be treated, and there are frequently psychological effects upon the cat. It cannot defend itself as ably as before if another cat picks a fight. Like the docking of tails and cropping of ears in dogs, it is a mutilation for the benefit of owners and is rarely indicated for medical reasons. Opposition to de-clawing is steadily growing in the United States, I'm glad to say.

Q *I love my houseplants and don't wish to get rid of them. How do I dissuade my cat from chewing them?*

A You can buy special cat-repelling preparations from the pet shop, or Bitter Apple or Bitter Orange extracts can be applied to the plants' leaves. Dusting with a little cayenne pepper is also very effective.

Q *Living in the country, I am concerned that foxes, which are in abundance in the woods nearby, might catch and kill my cat when he is out of the house. Is it likely?*

A No, it is not at all likely. I know of no authenticated case of a fox killing a cat. Cats are well able to defend themselves against an animal not that much bigger than themselves. The belief that foxes do kill and eat cats for food is based on occasional sightings of foxes chasing cats. This is usually in the spring, when the very young fox cubs are still underground. When inquisitive local cats come sniffing around, the vixen will chase them away from the earth but does not kill them. Later, in the summer, a band of the now older cubs will be out and about above ground exploring their neighbourhood, and, on occasion, they have been seen teasing a domestic cat, but there is never any fighting. The cubs know instinctively that a cat is not for tackling.

Q *Are there such things as hearing aids for deaf cats?*

A Yes, such devices have been developed in the USA and in Germany. Some cats, as you might imagine, don't like wearing them, but they do apparently improve the quality of life of stone-deaf animals. They aren't effective in all types of cat deafness. The aids are not yet readily available in British veterinary surgeries.

Q *My cat regularly vomits his food back. There is no sign of furballs, and the vet says there is no sign of a medical problem. Could it be behavioural?*

A This is a not uncommon phenomenon in cats, and it difficult to suggest a cause if stomach and bowel diseases and other medical conditions have been ruled out by your vet. The cause could be some constituent of its diet to which the cat is intolerant or, perhaps, the presence of a few hairs in the stomach, swallowed while grooming itself, even though no large accumulations in the form of hairballs are being seen. I suggest feeding small meals often and also trying one of the proprietary anti-furball cat foods now available.

Final thoughts...

So, having travelled together through the complex workings of the cat's mind, that intricate machine which controls it behaviour, attitudes and feelings, where are we at last? Certainly we cannot refer to the cat as a dumb animal in any sense of the word dumb. This animal is far from mute, possessing an extensive range of vocal as well as other sophisticated forms of communication. Even less is it dumb as signifying stupid in American usage.

A cat, each cat, is a unique, individual character. It reasons, it remembers, it has its loves and hates and, as we have seen, its dreams. Its appreciation of the world about it is different from ours, and in some ways more acute. It has made a success of walking out of the wild, tail up, as the lean hunting machine, and transforming itself into a companion animal in close association with mankind

But this renaissance has not entailed the animal losing its ancient knowledge or the innate skills of the solitary hunter of the jungle, forest or desert. This is no fawning, craven lickspittle. The Thinking Cat retains its essence, its free spirit, its dignity and, above all, its mysterious, inscrutable soul, where no man can see. I leave the last word to Charles Baudelaire, another great lover of cats.

> *Like those great sphinxes lounging through eternity in*
> *noble attitudes upon the desert sand, they gaze in curiosity*
> *at nothing, calm and wise.*

And, finally, readers can be assured that this book bears the imprimatur of Sidney, the senior cat in our family.

Appendix

Bach's flower essences

Many devotees of alternative medicine claim great success in handling a broad range of behavioural problems in cats by administering Bach's flower essences. These preparations, originally formulated for human use, are easily administered – four drops of the essence in the cat's drinking water each day – and are palatable and utterly safe. Many cats prefer water with essence in to water without. Other ways of giving the drops are directly into the mouth or rubbed into the skin of the throat or behind the ears. In emergencies, this can be repeated as often as every quarter of an hour.

They can be given alongside orthodox veterinary treatment but should never be regarded as a substitute for the latter where physical illness is involved. For emergency use, the well-known floral Rescue Remedy is recommended where a cat has been subjected to crisis, shock or any kind of physical trauma. How these essences might work is not known, and many orthodox medical and veterinary practitioners regard them as quackery. But owners have reported significant effects on their pets, and it can't be auto-suggestion ('all in the mind'): even the Thinking Cat knows nothing about alternative treatments and he can't read!

- **Abuse, neglect**: A mixture of Aspen, Larch Pine and Star of Bethlehem.
- **Aggressiveness**: Snapdragon or, if motivated by fear, Cherry Plum.
- **Aloofness**: Water violet.
- **Apathy**: (beware this is not associated with a medical condition) Wild Rose.
- **Bad habits in general**: Chestnut Bud.
- **Changed circumstances, surroundings or composition of household**: Beech and Walnut.
- **Fear**: Mimulus, Rock Rose, Aspen and Sweet Chestnut.
- **Grieving**: Honeysuckle.
- **Nervousness**: Impatiens.
- **Jealousy**: Holly.
- **Undue submissiveness**: Centaury and Larch.
- **Constant vocalization**: White Chestnut.

Alternative practitioners will give advice as to the precise kind of essence to use in any given individual cat after discussing its history with the owner. The great thing about these flower essences is that, even if they do not prove to be effective in every case, they cannot cause any harm.

Index

Abyssinian 16, 52, 150, 157, 180, 183
Addison's Disease 93
Adrenal gland 67, 93
African serval 50
African wild cat 8, 16, 39, 42
Ageing 78–87, 105–107
Aggression 92, 128, 129, 134–144, 161, 163–164, 167, 174, 180–181
Agoraphobia 130, 132
American Shorthair 183
Anabolic hormones 87
Anaemia 170
Angora 52
Antisocial cats 73
Anxiety 167–168, 176
Arthritis 51, 83, 85, 144
Asian leopard cat 56, 183
Asiatic desert cat 16
Aspirin 85
Aversion therapy 174, 176
Babies 72, 141, 166
Bach's Flower Essences 184, 189
Bad breath 110, 113–115
Balance 30–32, 91
Balinese 52
Bengal 52, 56, 183
  tiger 14
Birds 29
Birman 18, 20, 29, 44, 52, 107, 120, 180
Birth 56, 60–61
Biting 174, 177
Black-footed cat 8
Bladder disease 118
Blindness 81, 92, 108, 109–110
Boarding catteries 180
Bobcat 39, 63, 92
Body language 40–42
Body markings 39, 40
Bonding 60, 62
Boredom 70, 96, 170
Bowel disease 185
Brain 15, 31, 90–96, 105, 181
  degeneration 83

diseases of 93–95
  inflammation 92
  medical conditions, 91–92
  tumours 93, 144, 170
Bridging signal 153
Bronchitis 82
Burmese 16, 26, 52, 99, 157, 172
Calculus 113, 114
Camouflage 39
Cannibalism 142
Car travel 136, 151
Caracal lynx 27, 39, 50
Carnivores 14, 15, 24
Castration 66, 123, 181
Cat flap 6, 71, 76, 120
  training 155
Cataracts 81, 110
Catnip 24
Cave lion 16
Celestial navigation 35
Cheetah 9, 16, 27, 39, 61, 95
Chews 174
Chronic keratitis 110
Civet 15, 16
Claws 16, 112–113, 136, 151, 173, 185
Cleft palate 100
Clickes 153, 154
Climbing frames 11, 172
Coat patterns 39–40, 53
Colostrum 101
Colouration 39–40
Coma 92
Communication 39–45, 62
Competitive aggression, 134, 138–139
Conception 59
Congenital Cerebellar Hypoplasia 92
Constipation 111
Convulsions 91
Courtship 56, 58, 123
Creodonts 15
Crepuscular nature 6, 20
Cross-breeding 16, 56, 179, 180, 183
Cryptorchidism 125

Cystitis 82, 117
Deafness 23, 80–81, 99, 109–109, 186
Death 75, 87–88
De-clawing 185
Defecation 117
Dehydration 116
Dementia 92
Dental disease 113, 115
Depression 91, 92
Dermatitis 96
Dewclaws 110, 112
Diabetes 51, 67, 99, 115, 117, 170
Diarrhoea 25, 50, 117
Dieting 170
Disease aggression 144
Dissuasive training 155
Dogs 14, 15, 18, 27, 37, 72, 78, 136, 157–158, 159–161
Domestication 17–18
Dominant cats 11
Dreaming 6–7
Dried food 7, 116
Drinking 7
  problems 110, 115–116
Droppings 11
Ears 8–9, 22–23, 31, 39, 40, 79, 80, 95, 108–109, 151, 167, 186
  infections 109
  mites 108–109
Earthquakes 33
Egypt, Ancient 18, 75
Egyptian Mau 52
Elderly cats 7, 23, 38, 46, 47, 73, 78–87, 105–107, 117, 144, 157, 161–162
European wild cat 8, 42, 63
Euthanasia 34, 87–88
Evolution 15–16
Exercise 91
Eyes 6, 20–22, 31, 39, 40, 53, 57, 81, 109–110
Fabric chewing 98–99
False pregnancy 122–123, 126
Fear 127, 128, 129–133,

184
of prey 134
-provoked aggression 134, 135–137, 163, 167
Feeding 7, 47–52, 63, 76, 113–114
elderly cats 80
orphaned kittens 100–101
problems 167–171
Feline Cognitive Dysfunction 83
Feline Enteritis 92
Feline Hyperaesthesia 98
Feline Infectious Peritonitis 92
Feline Panleucopenia 92
Feline Spongiform Encephalopathy (FSE) 93–95
Feral cats 37, 71–72, 78
Fibre 170
Fighting 30, 163, 180
Fireworks 91
Fish 8
Fishing cat 8, 49, 178
Flat-headed cat 26, 49
Flehmen 24–25, 43
Fly catching 178
Food 47–52, 113–114, 116
Forest wild cat 16, 56
Foster mothers, 102, 103
Foxes 186
Fractures 32
Fur 46–47
Furballs 8, 110–112, 178, 185
Furniture scratching 173
Fussy eaters 168
Gait, staggering 92
Games 65
Gastrotomy 111
Gay cats 123–124
Genetic factors 53, 125
Gingivitis 113
Grass 8, 50, 177
boxes 50, 178
Grieving cats 75, 91, 167
Grooming 46, 47, 76, 82, 111, 142
Gum disease 113
Hair follicles 81
Handling 53, 64, 76, 107
Hearing 8–9, 19, 22–23, 79
aids 186
Heart problems 51, 82
Hermaphrodism 124
Hierarchies 68–71, 74, 138,

163
High-protein diet 181
Holidays 180
Home alone 172
Homeopathic remedies 133
Homing instinct 35–36
Homosexuality 123–124
Hopkins, Matthew 33
House cats 11, 72, 76, 77, 78, 91, 171, 184
House training 82, 147–150, 177
problems 85–86
Hormonal disturbances 92–93
Howling 176
Hunting 7, 9, 14, 22, 27–30, 63, 65, 139, 175, 180
technique 28
Hybrids 56, 183
Hydrocephalus 100
Hypersexuality 92, 122
Hyperthyroidism 93, 144
Hyposexualism 126
Hypothyroidism 93
Indoor cats 11, 72, 76, 77, 78, 91, 171, 184
Infanticide 58, 142
Infertility 126
Intelligence 36–38, 180
Intermittent reward system 154
Introducing cats 72–73, 158–159
Jacobson's organ 24
Jaguar 8, 16, 56, 142, 178
Jaws 9
Jealousy 140
Jungle cat 16
Kellas cat 56, 183
Kidney disease 117
Kills 29–30
Kittens 26, 32, 43, 45, 47–48, 53, 57, 60, 61–66, 76, 100–104, 139, 150, 157
Korat 16, 52
Labour 60
Larynx 45
Lead poisoning 99
Lead training 150–151
Lead walking 91
Learned aggression 143–144
Learning 37
Leopard 14, 28, 42, 43, 56,

64, 178
cat, 39
Life expectancy 78
Lion 29, 43, 50, 51, 56, 58, 64, 113, 124, 142, 171, 178
Litter 177
Litter size 57, 66
Litter trays 76, 86, 103, 117, 118–119, 147–148
Loneliness 70
Longhairs 110
Lynx 16, 27, 31, 39, 63
Maine Coon 52, 72, 125, 150
Male-on-male aggression 134–135
Manul 16
Manx 17, 31, 52
Margay 29, 183
Martelli's wild cat 16
Maternal instinct 141
Mating 56, 58, 59
aggression 141
Metabolic changes 81
Mexican hairless cat 17
Miacids 15
Middle Ear Disease 93
Milk 25, 100–101, 104, 123
Mite infestations 109
Mood detection 34–35
Moving house 119, 156–157, 171, 176, 184
Multi-cat households 52, 135, 147, 155
Munchkin 150
Muscle spasms 92
Musculo-skeletal system 83
Nails 42, 111
Natural selection 17
Nervous cats 130
Nervous system 6
Neutering 66–67, 69, 120, 123, 135, 137, 181
Newborn kittens 26, 32, 47
Night vision 20–21
Nocturnal behaviour 20–21
Norwegian Forest Cat 52, 150
Nutrient deficiency 50
Obesity 51, 67
preventing 170
Obsessive behaviour 96–100
Obsessive-compulsive behaviour 96–100, 111, 177
Ocelot 49, 92, 95, 142, 183
Ocicat 52, 183

Oestrogen 58, 122
Oestrus 24, 57, 58, 119, 122, 135
Omnivores 14
Oriental cats 57, 58, 98
Orphans 90, 100–104
Osteo-arthritis 85
Otitis Media 95
Ovarian cysts 122
Ovaries 57, 58
Overeating 51, 99, 170
Over-grooming 96–98, 111
Oviarectomy 66
Pain aggression 144
Panting 9
Parasites 30
Parental aggression 141–142
Patterns, coat 39–40, 53
Paws 28
Pedigree cats 18, 179
Peritonitis 108
Persecution 32–33
Persian 52, 172
Personality changes 91, 93, 105–108
Pet Passport Scheme 180
Petting aggression 142–143, 167, 174
Phantom pregnancy 122, 126
Phobias 128, 130–133
Pica 170
Plant eating 178, 179, 185
Play 64–66, 172
    aggression 140, 167
Poisoning 94–95, 99, 108
Poisonous plants 179
Predation aggression 139–140, 167
Pregnancy 56, 57, 59–60, 66, 109
    false 122, 126
Puma 28, 42, 51, 92, 95, 142
Purring 43, 45, 58
Quarantine 180
Rabies 92, 180
Ragdoll 52, 179
Recognition 182
Redirected aggression 144, 162, 167
Reproduction 56–61
Retinal disease 110
Rewards 152, 153
Rex 27, 52, 72, 172
Rheumatism 83, 119

Roaming 92, 107
Rodents 30, 49, 63, 180
Runaways 184
Russian Blue 52, 72, 150
Salmonellosis 30
Sand cat 7, 8
Scent 42–43, 69, 72
    marks 43, 111
    pheromones 158
Scottish Fold 52
Scratching, 9, 42, 69, 73, 111, 173, 182
    displays 51
    posts 11, 174
Scruffing 76
Sebaceous glands 42, 69, 81
Selective breeding 18
Self defence 163
Senses 15, 19
Serotonin 181
Sex 56–61
Shorthairs 52, 120, 150, 157
Siamese 17, 26, 29, 52, 63, 99, 100, 157, 172, 180, 183
Sight 19, 20–22, 81
Singapura 52
Skin 81–82
    disease 46, 177
    tumours 82
Sleep 6, 7, 86, 122, 176
Smell 19, 23–25, 43, 79
Sniffing 42
Somali 52
Speed 27
Sperm count 57
Sphynx 150
Spraying 9, 69, 119, 121, 173, 174, 177, 181
Stalking 65, 175
Stamina 27
Stomach disease 185
Stress 96, 119, 171, 177
Submissive posture 42
Suckling 47, 61, 101
Sulphadiazine 87
Swimming 178
Tabby 39, 56
Tail 31, 39, 42, 63, 167, 182
    markings 39, 40
Tapetum lucidum 20
Tapeworm 30
Taste 19, 25–26, 79
Teeth 9, 40, 113–115, 136
    brushing 114

Territorial aggression 134, 137–138, 161, 163, 167
Territory marking 69, 92, 111, 173
Testosterone 93, 123, 135
Tetanus 108
Thyroid gland 93, 99, 144
    over-active 170
Tiger 14, 16, 23, 26, 27, 28, 39, 42, 43, 50, 56, 64, 113, 114, 178
Tigon 56
Timidity 184
Toilet accidents 117, 148
Toilet stimulating regime 103
Toilet training 82, 85–86, 147–150, 177
Tonkinese 52
Tortoise-shells 125–126
Touch 19, 26–27, 42
Toxic substances 94–95
Toxoplasma 177
Toys 172, 174, 175
Training 15, 38, 146–155
    dissuasive 155
Travelling containers 129, 136
Trembling 93
Turkish Van 52, 178
Undereating 99
Urinary problems 82
Urination 9, 10, 42, 43, 73, 82, 86, 91, 117–118
Valerian 24
Vet visits 129, 136, 137
Vibrations 32, 33, 45
Vision 6, 19, 20–22, 34, 81
Visitors 73, 130
Vitamins 8, 80, 87, 99, 169
Vocalization 43–44, 58, 176
Voice 43
Volcanic eruptions 33
Vomiting 50, 185
Walking on lead 91, 150–151
Water 7, 115, 116
Weaning 47–48
Weight 51, 67, 93, 170
    loss 93, 111, 170
Whiskers 26–27, 40, 42, 183
Wild cats 14, 16, 17, 26, 42, 61, 64, 99, 114, 175, 178, 183
Wool sucking 98, 99, 171
Word recognition 23
Xenophobia 131, 133

Useful addresses

Cats Protection
17 Kings Road
Horsham
West Sussex RH13 5PN
Tel: 01403 221900
Fax: 01403 218414

The Association of Pet Behaviour Counsellors
PO Box 46
Worcester WR8 9YS
Tel: 01386 751151
Fax: 01386 751151

The Feline Advisory Bureau
Taeselbury
High Street
Tisbury
Wiltshire SP3 6LZ
Tel: 01747 871872
Fax: 01747 871873

Wood Green Animal Shelters
Heydon
Royston
Herts SG8 8PN
Tel: 01763 838829

The Governing Council of the Cat Fancy
4-7 Penel Orlieu
Bridgewater
Somerset TA6 3PG
Tel: 01278 427575
Fax: 01278 446627